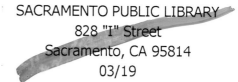

PENGUIN BOOKS

SO MUCH LONGING IN SO LITTLE SPACE

Karl Ove Knausgaard's first novel, *Out of the World*, was the first ever debut novel to win the Norwegian Critics' Prize, and his second, *A Time for Everything*, was widely acclaimed. The *My Struggle* cycle of novels has been heralded as a masterpiece wherever it has appeared, and the first volume was awarded the prestigious Brage Prize.

D0019450

Also by Karl Ove Knausgaard

SO MUCH LONGING IN SO LITTLE SPACE

THE ART OF EDVARD MUNCH

KARL OVE KNAUSGAARD

Translated from the Norwegian by Ingvild Burkey

Penguin Books

PENGUIN BOOKS
An imprint of Penguin Random House LLC
penguinrandomhouse.com

Published simultaneously in the United States by Penguin Books,
an imprint of Penguin Random House LLC and in Great Britain by Harvill Secker,
an imprint of Penguin Random House Limited 2019

Originally published under the title *Så mye lengsel på så liten flate. En bok om
Edvard Munchs bilder* in Norway by Forlaget Oktober in 2017.

This book was published with the financial assistance of NORLA
(Norwegian Literature Abroad).

This book was written following Karl Ove Knausgaard's collaboration with
the Munch Museum on the exhibition *Towards the Forest – Knausgaard on Munch*,
Oslo, May 6–October 8 2017.

Credits for paintings appear on pages 245–6.

LIBRARY OF CONGRESS CATALOGING-IN-PUBLICATION DATA
Names: Knausgêard, Karl Ove, 1968- author. | Burkey, Ingvild, 1967–translator.
Title: So much longing in so little space : the art of Edvard Munch / Karl
   Ove Knausgaard ; translated from the Norwegian by Ingvild Burkey.
Other titles: Sêa mye lengsel pêa sêa liten flate. English
Description: London : Harvill Secker ; New York : Penguin Books, 2019.
Identifiers: LCCN 2018057501 (print) | LCCN 2018058011 (ebook) |
   ISBN 9780525504900 (ebook) | ISBN 9780143133131 (paperback)
Subjects: LCSH: Munch, Edvard, 1863–1944--Criticism and interpretation. |
   BISAC: ART / Individual Artists / General. | ART / Criticism & Theory. |
   LITERARY CRITICISM / European / Scandinavian.
Classification: LCC ND773.M8 (ebook) | LCC ND773.M8 K6313 2019 (print) |
   DDC 759.81--dc23
LC record available at https://lccn.loc.gov/2018057501

Printed in the United States of America
10 9 8 7 6 5 4 3 2 1

Set in Scala OT

For Sissel

Sometimes it is impossible to say why and how a work of art achieves its effect. I can stand in front of a painting and become filled with emotions and thoughts, evidently transmitted by the painting, and yet it is impossible to trace those emotions and thoughts back to it and say, for example, that the sorrow came from the colours, or that the longing came from the brushstrokes, or that the sudden insight that life will end lay in the motif.

One picture I feel this way about was painted by Edvard Munch in 1915. It depicts a cabbage field. The cabbages in the foreground are roughly executed, almost sketch-like, dissolving into green and blue brushstrokes deeper into the background. Next to the cabbage field there is an area of yellow, over that an area of dark green, and over that again a narrow band of darkening sky.

That is all, that is the whole painting.

But the picture is magical. It is so charged with meaning, looking at it I feel as if something is bursting within me. And yet it is just a field of cabbages.

So what is going on with this painting?

When I look at its colours and shapes, which are so radically simplified that they suggest a landscape more than they represent it, I see death, as if the painting intended a reconciliation with death, but a trace of something terrible remains, and what is terrible is the unknown, that we don't know what awaits us.

But Munch's painting doesn't really say anything, doesn't give form to anything other than cabbages, grain, trees and sky. And yet death, and yet reconciliation, and yet peace, and yet a trace of something terrible.

Is it simply that the line of the field leads inwards, towards darkness, and that dusk is descending in the sky above?

Perhaps. But many have painted fields, many have painted dusk, without attaining what this painting so calmly radiates.

Munch was around fifty years old when he painted *Cabbage Field.* He was known as a painter of the inner life, of dream, death and sexuality. He had gone through a life crisis, after that he withdrew from social life, and he no longer sought out pain when he painted, he turned out-wards, he painted the sun. And that isn't hard to understand, everything begins anew when the sun rises. Darkness yields, the day opens up, the world once again becomes visible. Over the next thirty years he painted what he saw there, in the visible world. But the visible world is not objective reality, it appears to each individual as seen by them, and Munch's great gift lay in his ability to paint not only what his gaze took in, but also what that gaze was charged with.

There is a longing in this painting of the cabbage field, a longing to disappear and become one with the world. And that longing to disappear and become one with the world fulfilled the painting for him, fulfilled for him the act of painting. That is why this painting is so good, what disappears re-emerges in what comes into being, and if the disappearance ceased for the painter as soon as he finished the painting, it is still represented in the picture, which fills us again and again with its emptiness.

Cabbages. Grain and forest.

Yellow and green, blue and orange.

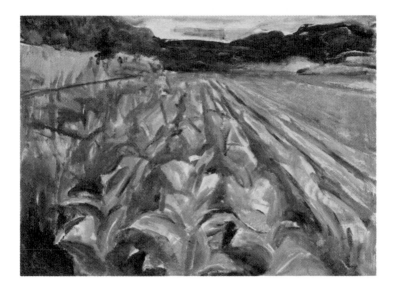

ONE

Edvard Munch painted all his life, from his teenage years, when he produced small pictures of potted plants and interiors, portraits of family members and exteriors near the place where he grew up, until he died at Ekely, eighty years old, surrounded by his works. The constant activity which painting was for him can be divided into different phases, the first being his apprentice years, during which he painted himself into tradition, initially by producing youthfully clumsy landscapes and portraits, followed surprisingly quickly by confident and good paintings, culminating in a qualitative break which was also his first masterpiece, *The Sick Child*, in 1885–6. He was twenty-two years old. The second was the period up to 1892, when he painted in many styles and was clearly searching for a way to give expression to what he had within him; the canvases from this period include everything from realistic harbour motifs to classically Impressionist street scenes. The third phase is the one we think of as 'Munchian' – this is when he painted *Melancholy, Vampire, The Scream, Evening on Karl Johan Street, Death in the Sickroom, Puberty, Anxiety, Madonna, Jealousy*. The fourth phase began around the turn of the century, when he abandoned symbolist language and thinking and took his by then distinctive style and method into something else, less literary and more painterly, even as he returned to painting earlier motifs at regular intervals up until his death in 1944.

Of course there are no walls between these phases. Throughout his career, for example, he painted full-length portraits that are hardly affected by developments in the rest of his work, and he continually painted self-portraits up until the end, which belong among his best works. The long final phase itself contained a number of periods which it is possible to delimit, such as the vitalistic period, when he painted naked men and bathers, horses and labourers, or the monumental period, when he worked on various public art commissions, of which the mural *The Sun* in the assembly hall of Oslo University remains a high point.

To divide an artist's productive life into phases is a way of handling it, and this feels especially important in Munch's case, since the works he is now remembered for are almost exclusively paintings dating to a particular period, numbering some ten to fifteen paintings out of a total production of more than 1,700, so familiar by now that they have become emblems of themselves and therefore almost impossible to see as anything other than that. The style refers to Munch, and Munchian refers to the style, in a circular movement that closes the paintings off to the viewer, shutting us out. That movement belongs to modernity, the age of reproduction; along with van Gogh's sunflowers and Monet's water-lily ponds, Picasso's *Guernica* and Matisse's dancing women, Munch's *The Scream* is perhaps the most iconic image of our time. This means that the picture has invariably already been seen, so it is no longer possible to see it as if for the first time, and since so much of what Munch invested in this painting had to do precisely with alienation, with seeing the world as if for the first time by creating a distance of non-familiarity, it is clear that *The Scream* is in a sense ruined for us as a work of art.

But Munch as an artist is not ruined. His production was so huge, and so little of it has been exhibited, that it is still possible to approach his pictures with fresh eyes. And by not focusing exclusively on his masterpieces, by not stopping at them but rather seeing them as stations along a more than sixty year long continual search for meaning, a continual exploration of the world through painting, full of failure, fumbling and banality but also of wildness, audacity and triumph, perhaps *The Scream* too will come into its own as a work of art, that is to say, be seen as something oscillating between the ridiculous and the fantastic, between the perfected and the unfinished, the beautiful and the ugly, painted in a small town on the world's periphery, at the junction between the old and the new, at the very dawn of the era which would become our own.

*

As a person Munch was emotional, nervous and self-absorbed, and as an artist he was lucky, in that he was noticed at the very beginning of his career and was helped in ways that fairly quickly locked him into painting, which at first was as much a way of being seen as a way of seeing, and which eventually became a way of life, the only one he knew. He never did anything other than paint, he never held a job, he didn't found a family, and he hardly spent any time on the practical matters which a life is usually full of. So in many ways Munch's life was extreme – extremely monomaniacal, extremely dedicated, extremely solitary. But it was in no way heroic, it was as much a matter of hiding or fleeing from the world and its challenges as of renouncing security and accepting the cost of creating something unique. Munch may have lacked a basic human quality, that of becoming attached to other people, of living in a close relationship to others. Reading biographies it becomes clear that he had a great fear of intimacy, and just as clear why: he lost his mother when he was five years old, and he lost his older sister, to whom he was very attached, when he was thirteen. His father died when Edvard was twenty-five, his younger brother when he was thirty-two, and in a sense he lost even his sister Laura, who became seriously mentally ill at an early age. If to this series of losses one adds an acute sensitivity and a distant, at times religiously confused, partly kindly and partly brutal father figure during his youth, one ends up with a child, a teenager and a grown man who is so afraid of losing that he deals with it by simply not acquiring. In time, Munch would assiduously avoid places within himself that might prove painful, it became a life strategy. When his mother's sister, who had been almost a mother to him, died towards the end of his life, he didn't attend the funeral but witnessed it from a distance. He stood outside the churchyard wall, looking in.

How important is such information when we look at his pictures? This is a crucial question in regard to Munch's art, but also in regard to art generally. There is obviously a connection between an artist's personal experiences and his or her works, but it is rather less obvious what this connection might consist of. Did Picasso paint the way he did because of his relationship to his parents, because of the circumstances in which he grew up, due to his unique inner life? To claim this would be an absurd reduction of Picasso's *oeuvre*, and completely insensitive towards the problems he set out to resolve as he faced a blank canvas. The same is true of authors, whose biographies naturally play a part in the writing of their books, but in ways that can seldom be traced back directly – think of Hermann Broch's novel *The Death of Virgil* (1945), for example, or a film like *Solaris* (1972) by Andrei Tarkovsky, to mention two distinctive works of the previous century in which biographical elements play a minimal role in understanding or experiencing them but which are nevertheless personal in the sense that it is difficult to imagine them having been created by anyone other than Broch and Tarkovsky.

A work of art is like a point in a system of three coordinates: the particular place, the particular time, the particular person. The more time has passed since the creation of a work, the more apparent it becomes that individuality, the particular person's experiences and psychology, plays less of a role than the culture in which it found expression. I am sure that a well-informed and competent reader in the Middle Ages would have been able to distinguish between different book illustrators of that time, and that the differences between illustrators were perhaps even considered essential, while for us, at least for me, the style expresses one thing and one thing only: the medieval.

An example nearer to our time might be the work of Norwegian author Dag Solstad, which extends from the 1960s until today and in which the literary aesthetics of successive decades always resonate, so that in *Patina! Green!* we hear the tone of the 60s, in *September 25th Square* the tone of the

70s, in *High School Teacher Pedersen's Account of the Great Political Awakening that Has Swept Our Nation* the tone of the 80s, in *Shyness and Dignity* the tone of the 90s, in *Armand V. Footnotes to An Unexcavated Novel* the tone of the 2000s. What is interesting is that Solstad's own, original and highly idiosyncratic voice is also present throughout these five decades, one need only read a sentence or two from any one of these novels to ascertain that he wrote them. When *Patina! Green!* was first published, it was that voice which stood out clearly, while the novel's air of the 1960s was in the background, almost unperceived. Now its 1960s-ness is the first thing we notice, and Dag Solstad's voice is more in the background.

This is so because we see the world without being aware of our way of seeing it, those two things are often one and the same to us. It feels as if we are living in an unmediated reality, and when someone mediates it for us, which is what artists do, they often portray it in ways that correspond so closely to our own perception of reality that we confuse them too. This applies to what we pay attention to and consider essential, it applies to notions we hold about people and the world, it applies to the use of language and imagery. If we look at a daily TV newscast from 1977, for example, we notice at once the clothes, which are different in ways that often make us smile, and the hairdos and the spectacles. We notice the way people express themselves, which seems stiffer and more formal than what we are used to now, and we notice the unbelievably parochial and innocent news coverage. But back then, in 1977, no one noticed any of this. The tone of the 1970s didn't exist, because everything and everyone belonged to the 70s, everyone shared the style of clothing, the hairdos, the design of the spectacles, the manner of speech, the field of interest. All of this is part of a shared space, it is what we call the zeitgeist, the spirit of the time, which is also what we express ourselves through. A poor novel will express only this, regardless of whether it relies on personal experiences and perhaps describes events that the author has actually lived through, and after some years it will have no other value than as a document of the time.

That culture is seen as nature, and that judgements and notions which are arbitrary and time-bound are unconsciously perceived as timelessly true, falls within the rhetorical concept of *doxa*, and it was underlying notions such as these that Roland Barthes charted and described in his book *Mythologies*. When I studied at university in the early 1990s, this was the dominant thinking, French philosophy held the ascendancy in academia, and this has influenced my view of time and art, presumably also in ways I myself am unaware of. To me, the most important theorist by far was Michel Foucault, in particular his book *The Order of Things*, which felt like a revelation when I read it for the first time. Yes, *that's* how it is! I thought then, and I still think so. And of course what I am writing here, both the way I write it and the thoughts I express through it, are also a part of the zeitgeist, also belong to notions that I now feel to be true, for this is what reality looks like to me, so it is highly likely that this too will one day express merely the time- and place-specific.

I think this is why so many artists and writers talk about truth, say that they want to express what is true. In this conception truth is seen as lying behind something else, there is always a veil of notions that must be pulled aside in order for us to see the truth, to see the world as it really is. And to do that one must possess a language other than the language of one's time, since the language of the age is one of the things that conceal or overshadow. This is why originality is among the most highly valued qualities in the world of art. Originality is the idiosyncratic, the particular, it is the new. Whereas the true is always the same.

The first painting we know Munch admired, when he was still a child, was *Bridal Procession on the Hardangerfjord* by Adolph Tidemand and Hans Gude. In his late teens he developed a strong aversion to such paintings, with their numerous photorealistic details and glossy surfaces, and it is hardly a wild speculation to claim that this aversion arose out of his personal experiences, which in no way corresponded to the image of reality created by these paintings: of connection, balance, beauty and meaning. When his mother died, he became closely attached to his sister Sophie, it was the two of them together, they shared a world of their own, and he was the sick one, he was the one coughing blood and lying in bed during the winter months, whereas it was she who died, suddenly, following a summer when he had been in love with one of her girlfriends, it was over in a few weeks, she grew weaker and weaker and died in the chair in front of the window, their father Christian and aunt Karen carried her dead body to the bed, and Edvard was the one who went on living. He never quite got over her loss, he longed for Sophie the rest of his life. The basic trust in others and in the world that most of us have must have been shattered for him. One of his biographers, Sue Prideaux, believes that he dealt with the trauma by withdrawing into himself, thus severing the connection between the internal and the external world, a rupture which eventually became permanent. He lived out his inner life through reading and drawing, and his drawings met with so much approval early on that he must have come to base his identity on his art. Later, when as a young man who thought of himself as an artist he viewed Norwegian romantic paintings, which were almost the only paintings in existence in Kristiania at the time, he saw nothing that represented his own reality and experience, and he understood early on that he would have to break with the embellishment which stood between the images of reality and what he perceived as real if he was to accomplish something true, something consequential. He read Ibsen, whose works sought to tear down the embellished facade in order to find the truth, and he read Dostoevsky, who against a background of poverty and imperfection and unbearable inner pain brought forth in his writing something luminous, shining, burning. He met the painter Christian Krohg, who returned from Paris as a great and disruptive force and almost single-handedly implanted impulses from abroad into the small Norwegian art scene, and who questioned the relevance of seventeenth-century baroque pastoral painting for modern life in nineteenth-century Norway. And he met the writer Hans Jæger, who spoke not only of the hypocrisy and inhibition of the bourgeoisie but about describing one's life as openly and honestly and nakedly and truthfully as possible. That Jæger himself proved to be a hypocrite didn't diminish the value of what Munch learned from him, and he was later to say that Jæger, not Strindberg, had been his most powerful influence; by the time he met Strindberg, his most important ideas had already been formed.

*

Such refractions between the individual and the cultural, both being time-bound entities, occur in all works of art. The artist strives for truth by liberating him- or herself from time and place, the dominant language, at the same time as he or she is involuntarily a part of it, because the timeless and the placeless simply don't exist, even the most original work of art and the most original thought are bound to time and place. In this sense there is an ironic dimension to the history of art; only those works that break with the era come to be seen as typical of the era, those works in which the artist's personal vision forces its way through, using the language and the methods then available to and belonging to everybody. That is why the works of Albrecht Dürer and Dante Alighieri remain relevant to us, while so many other works of the Middle Ages are not. By expressing their own self they speak to what we have in common with them, namely our self. This 'own self' was once linked to a very particular character formed by a set of very particular experiences, but time has faded it until all that remains is a certain tone, a certain attitude to the language and form available, that to us is almost indistinguishable from the time in which it was formulated.

Edvard Munch's time is still so close to our own that his biography has not yet vanished into his paintings, so we continue to seek the causes of his idiosyncrasies, what enabled him to break with the art of his contemporaries, in his personality and personal experiences. He lost his mother and sister as a child, and he was exceptionally sensitive, that is why he painted *The Scream*.

But why did Dürer paint the portrait of himself as Christ? Most critics interpret it against the wider cultural-historical background, including the German philosopher Peter Sloterdijk, who sees the painting as a strangely concrete expression of 'the elevation of the profane face to a subject worthy of portraiture'. This is at the transition between the Middle Ages and the Renaissance, the turning away from belief in the truth of canonised texts towards the truth found in nature, and that is a place where the question of whether Dürer's mother or any of his siblings died when he was a child has no relevance, even if his self-portrait seems just as personal and deeply felt as Munch's.

What it is possible to say in a given epoch, and how it can be said, defines more than anything the different expressions of art, and this of course applies to Munch too. That during the 1890s he began to paint scenes from his own life, and that he sought to give external painterly form to his inner emotions, was not solely the result of intense inner pressure – I assume that most major painters throughout history have experienced intense inner pressure – but also because something in the culture changed, opening that possibility for him.

That Munch began only ten years later to move away from the method he had found and for the rest of his life, that is to say close on forty years, produced very different paintings, which are rarely charged with either biography or strong emotion, means, I think, that what interested and drove him was never merely the biographical or his own inner life per se, but also what it might yield in terms of art. Perhaps even primarily the latter.

After ten years the method had been emptied out, in other words it became recognisable as just that, a method, and no longer yielded anything new, but instead entailed repetition and restatement, exactly what he must have felt that the rules of painting, which he had been trained to observe and which were all around him when he first began to paint, represented. That which is present beforehand, before one even picks up the paintbrush.

*

The conflict between what is present beforehand and what comes into being without precedent, was fundamental to Munch, it was a battle he waged, resulting in both great victories and great defeats. The irony is that the pictures he is remembered for do not process merely memories, that is, work with past events, but also states of mind and emotional conflicts which the elements of the picture are tasked to bring out, so that some of them are less in themselves than what they signify – the painting *Jealousy* might serve as one example, with its formulaic Adam and formulaic Eve with apples in the background and a pale, suffering face in the foreground, in which the figures appear to have been placed following a set formula, as an illustration of the emotion, in a painting that doesn't have much more to offer than that – while the paintings where he succeeded, by approaching what he was painting almost entirely without bias – an elm is an elm, a hay-drying rack is a hay-drying rack, a horse is a horse – but not in strict accordance with the rules of art, not at all, but instead hastily and often carelessly, emphasising their paintedness – an overtly painted elm, an overtly painted hay-drying rack, an overtly painted horse – these are largely considered an insignificant part of his *oeuvre*.

'It is a mistake to think that the painter works on a white

surface,' Gilles Deleuze writes in his book about the Irish-British painter Francis Bacon. By this he means that one can never simply transfer a motif to an empty canvas, because the canvas is never empty but filled with images and notions the painter already carries within himself, so that painting is really more about emptying, cleansing, removing things, than about filling a blank surface. The painter paints 'in order to produce a canvas whose functioning will reverse the relations between model and copy. In short, what we have to define are those "givens" [*données*] that are on the canvas before the painter's work begins, and determine, among those givens, which are an obstacle, which are a help, or even the effects of a preparatory work.'[1]

This is the starting position, the basis for all painterly activity, and actually for all other forms of artistic production too, including writing, if not in quite the same way. Deleuze called this chapter 'The painting before painting', and that which is always there beforehand, standing between the painter and the motif even before he begins to paint, is on the one hand cliché and all it entails, on the other hand possibility and all it entails. To paint is to enter into the cliché and into possibility, and, Deleuze writes, the painter enters into the painting precisely because he knows what he wants to do but not how to do it, and the only path to that certainty leads through the painting and out of it.

For Munch as a young man in Kristiania, cliché – the idiom most immediately at his disposal – was not those romantic, pedantically painted pictures, those he had already put behind him, but naturalism's more realistic contemporary paintings. The possibilities – in other words, what he wanted and in some way or other imagined or sensed – must for their part have been tied to his own experiences and to his encounter with Dostoevsky's brutally direct depiction of the outer world, seen through or tempered by the inner. The conflict must have been intense, since the divergence between Munch's inner life and the external reality he moved in appears to have been so comprehensive.

When we view an artist's *oeuvre* in retrospect, one phase succeeds the other with a certain naturalness, since we already know what is coming, and that certainty can never be entirely disregarded. But for the artist nothing was obvious at the time, all that existed was what had already been painted and what was just then being painted. As the eighteen-year-old Munch stands painting a garden on a lovely summer day, he knows nothing about *The Scream*, he knows nothing about *Melancholy*, he knows nothing about *The Sun* or *Elm Forest in Spring*. If there is a conflict within him between the internal and the external, it isn't articulated, nor is it necessarily the case that this conflict points to something further ahead. The painting is more than a place where inner conflicts are given expression, it is also a place where these conflicts are bearable, that is, a place of peace and joy. To paint is to see and to articulate what is seen in colours and shapes. That is what Munch did as he stood before that garden: he looked at it, and he painted what he saw. Nothing of the trauma he carried within is represented in the picture, but his ability to see is, and his ability to transpose what he sees into a painting.

Konsten att se, the art of seeing, is the Swedish title of art critic and novelist John Berger's book *Ways of Seeing* (1972). And that might sound odd, for don't we all know how to see? Hardly an art, is it? Each of us can stand in front of a tree and look at it, its branches and leaves, its bark and roots, the play of light and shadow which seems to sift down upon the lawn it grows in when the sea breeze makes it sway back and forth. But much of what we see, we see because we know it is there, often it is more a matter of recognition, of registering something which already exists within us. Names play an important role in this, so much of what we see lies in the name; that is an apple tree, that is an elm, that is a cherry tree, that is a spruce. If we look at it for longer, we might get beneath the name and see it as a unique, singular tree and not merely as a representative of the category it belongs to. And eventually we may even be able to see what it 'is', its presence in the world. But by then we will have come to know it so well that it will seem familiar to us, which in turn creates a distance, for that's how it is with the familiar, isn't it, friends we've known for years – we no longer see them, we just note their presence, allowing it to fill the category we have created for them.

If we were to paint that tree, not only would all the different ways of seeing it lie between us and the tree, but also all the different ways of depicting it. The trees of the baroque, the trees of Impressionism, the trees of naturalism, the trees of Symbolism, the trees of modernism and postmodernism, van Gogh's trees, David Hockney's trees, Anna Bjerger's trees, Peter Doig's trees, Vanessa Baird's trees. But also the trees of natural science books, the trees of brochures advertising banking services, the trees in video games, the trees photographed for newspapers and magazines, the trees of nature programmes on TV, the trees of children's drawings.

'Many had painted oaks before,' Olav H. Hauge wrote in a poem. 'Nevertheless Munch painted an oak.' The line captures the essence of Edvard Munch's work, since it says so much about why he painted, what he was attempting to do. And the way he painted trees can be as good an entry point as any to his art, for he painted trees from his very first painting in 1880 until his last in 1944, and faced with each and every one of them he found himself in the situation described by Deleuze: the battle between cliché and possibility, of which the painting is the outcome.

One of Munch's first good paintings is *Garden With Red House* from 1882, the summer he was eighteen. The format is small, only 23 by 30.5 centimetres, the motif is a garden in summer, lush foliage and grass flooded with sunlight, in many nuances of green, with a red cottage beneath a blue sky in the background, which sets up a yearning within the painting and also a sense of pleasure, for if his ambition in painting was perhaps a modest one and extended no further than a wish to master the motif and his joy in the colours and the light, it works nevertheless; it is difficult to look at the painting and not feel uplifted.

In the very foreground, at the lower left edge of the painting, stands the leafless trunk of a tree, it appears to have been an old fruit tree, covered here and there by mint-green moss, elsewhere light grey where it reflects the sun, dark grey where it lies in shadow. Next to it there is a grey bench and a table that looks rust-red in the shade, both appear rickety, and behind them there is a lawn, luminous in the sunlight, wreathed by dense foliage and opulent flower beds, yellow by the wall of the house, three distinctly red flowers at the right edge of the painting. Both motif and atmosphere are impressionistic, while the execution is heavier and has the solidity of naturalism but without naturalism's sometimes almost hyperrealistic reproduction of detail. The main thing here is colour, colour and depth.

What was 'the painting before painting' here? What images were in his mind before he began painting, and which possibilities did he see?

Presumably the only thing he really wanted was to make the painting cohere, based on what he had learned in the two years since he had begun to paint and on the pictures he had seen in the form accessible to him, which was realism or naturalism. There is no trace of national romanticism in the picture, which some of his earlier paintings in some ways come close to with their birches and small peasant figures in the foreground. Munch never painted tall mountains, never deep valleys, never fjords or landscapes that were dramatic in other ways. Here too it isn't grandeur he is after, rather it must have been the very insignificance of the motif that attracted him, and the beauty or charm it possessed. If he was content simply to be able to represent the garden and give form to the old fruit tree as he saw it, and found no reason to reject the prevailing painterly means, but instead worked hard to achieve them, such as the depth of the garden, the volume of the tree trunk, the connections between light and colour, then the delight in colour, or the desire for it, must at some point have taken over, for that is what predominates in this painting, the physicality of colour more than what the colour represents: the sunlit red of the cottage, the shady red of the table, the three flower heads, also red, amid a sea of green.

I don't think it is possible to paint a painting like this without being light-hearted, full of the joy of living. It may be that I am naive, and that it certainly is possible, but I for one am unable to look at this painting without being affected by its peaceful mood and contagious thirst for colour.

If we consider a picture he painted eleven years later, at the age of twenty-nine, *Summer Night's Dream (The Voice)*, which also has a summery outdoor motif with trees as a key element, it is so different in all its aspects that it is difficult to grasp that it was made by the same man. The painting shows a white-clad female figure who appears to be leaning against a tree; behind her, between tree trunks, lies the sea, above it, roughly in the middle of the picture, hangs the moon, mirrored in a column in the water, and to the right a boat is glimpsed. That is all. The elements are realistic in the sense that they belong to visible reality, but they are painted so differently from the elements in the sun-dappled summer garden that something very different is clearly at stake here from a painterly and thematic point of view. The forest floor in the foreground is a nearly even field of dark green, the beach in the middle distance is a nearly even field of white with a red border, and the sea in the background is a perfectly even field of blue. The trees are flat, practically without volume. The painting therefore has hardly any depth, and it is clear that the pictorial space is not a realistic one. It lives in the play between the horizontal lines of beach and sea and the obtrusive, grid-like verticality of the trees, which is intensified or deepened by the column of moonlight. This should have made the painting verge on the abstract and the decorative, turning it into a thing to be contemplated from a distance, quite unlike the realistic garden scene, which comes to life by being convincing and recognisable. But that is not the case. Even if it doesn't quite cancel out the various elements of the painting, the woman's presence and pose puts them into play in a different way. She is standing with her hands behind her back while bending forward slightly, looking straight at the viewer. In the painting she is alone, but it doesn't feel like a picture of a woman alone by the sea, on the contrary, the picture is emotionally charged in the manner of a scene, everything about her posture and body language indicates that there is someone else there, to whom she is turning. Looking at the picture, it is impossible not to become this figure and in that way be forced to confront her directly. It is me she is looking at, it is me she is leaning towards. And it is me she frightens.

Frightens?

What is it about her that could possibly be frightening?

Am I reading what I know about Munch into the painting, his dread of intimacy and his fear of involving himself with women, and simply making it my own, which isn't difficult, since both dread of intimacy and fear of women are familiar to me?

That may well be.

But the space of the painting has no depth, so that it doesn't open, and the trees stand there like the bars of a cage, blocking the way, shutting one in. And in Munch's pictorial world trees and verticality are masculine entities, while the sea and the horizontal are feminine.

She is appealing to someone, someone who is looking at her, and the invitation suggested by her posture, this play-acting directed at the viewer, makes her a siren-like figure. Understood in this way, the painting opens a space where desire and destruction are juxtaposed.

It is as if in this picture Munch has painted not only the woman, but also the person looking at the woman. And the picture therefore changes depending on the experience of the viewer. Of course one might object that this applies to all pictures, even one of a garden, but this particular picture is confrontational in quite another way, it demands something of the viewer, who is forced to respond. It is not that the male gaze, with which I approach the painting, sexualises the woman and dominates her, it is more complicated than that, for this woman is free, she is connected with the open and the unbound, and if one sets aside the obvious erotic over-tones of the painting, freedom is also a choice the viewer is forced to confront. Since no choice has been made in the painting, it is also full of longing. Yes, it is as if longing itself is its real subject.

But what was 'the painting before painting' here? What images were in his head before he began to paint, what stood in his way, and which possibilities did he see?

Almost everything he had learned about painting stood in his way here; everything he knew about creating volume and building up space with light, whatever connected it with a particular moment in time and thereby gave the painting a presence both contemporaneous and convincing, all this he had to ignore. What he wanted, the possibility he saw, was to paint a memory, in other words not the world as he saw it but as he remembered it. But not just any memory, not an insig-nificant and everyday episode – as the garden was an insignificant and everyday garden – but a memory which in some way or other was essential, expressing something over and beyond itself about something that was always the case. What is always the case exists outside of time, so he didn't need any of the things that connected the motif with time, nor anything that connected it to visible space, for what he was after was the space of memory. The trees become signposts for trees, the boat becomes a signpost for boat, the moon becomes a signpost for moon, the woman becomes a signpost for woman. The objects relate to reality because memory relates to reality, but this relation isn't binding. Munch is clearly painting his own longing, desire and fear when confronted with the feminine, or perhaps confronted with life, what it means to be truly alive, based on a memory of something that happened to him one night in Åsgårdstrand, but the almost wild reduction of detail obliterates everything that initially linked the memory to himself and to the actual place.

To have the skill to paint a tree trunk with convincing naturalism and instead choose to merely indicate it with a couple of brushstrokes of brown paint, in this lies a freedom but also the potential for new compulsion, for if one does it a few times, paints trees in that way, this soon becomes the image one has transferred to the canvas before one even begins to paint, against which one has to struggle.

If we now consider some of the trees Munch painted in the final phase of his life, for example in a painting called *Elm Forest in Spring* from the mid-1920s, we are once again transported to a radically different pictorial language. The motif is leafless trees in a forest, and as with the painting of the garden this picture is devoid of people, but unlike it there is no sky here and nothing in it is man-made. A red-orange forest floor, greyish trees with touches of bright green, most of them gnarled and crooked, some more upright in the background, where they blend and merge into vague blue-grey stripes. This space is even more closed up than the one in front of the beach, yet it doesn't feel claustrophobic to me, presumably because it isn't charged with anything human, no situation, no memories, no romance, no sexual drive or dread of intimacy. The garden painting isn't charged with any of this either, but the human is still present in it through the objects left behind, the house and the garden – and perhaps the peacefulness of that painting derives precisely from the absence of people? The picture of the elm forest holds no such peace within it. It seems to hold nothing at all, really, it isn't charged with anything. The life of this painting lies in the tension between what it is a picture of, the shapes of the trees, the spring light upon them, and what the painting is in itself, its colours, forms and strokes of paint. The light is at one and the same time light and an orange layer of paint in which the brushstroke is clearly visible. The shadow on the dominant tree, which is an oak, is painted green, with a thin layer that appears to have run a little. We are very far from the naturalistic fruit tree in the garden, but also very far from the flat tree trunk signposts in the summer night painting.

What does this painting want with us?

It doesn't want anything. This picture is a matter between the painter and what he is painting. If it communicates anything, it communicates the way trees communicate. Without a word, through their presence, embodied through their form, as if infinitely slowly contorting. They don't mean anything, they are. And what they are, they are in a particular way. The trees in this painting are not masculinity, the forest is not death, nor is spring, heralded by the light, life. The forest is forest, the trees are trees, and this painting is a picture of them. The painter painting it does so almost selflessly, it is as if he is painting on the forest's terms. As a consequence, there isn't a great deal of meaning to be extracted from this picture, there isn't much to write about, because the picture is what it is, just as the trees are what they are.

Munch's method had been to use himself, not by painting what he saw but by trying to visualise what he felt while seeing, so that even a picture of a snow-covered, deserted forest was charged with loneliness and longing, but in the end he came here, to a place where he cancelled out himself and didn't invest more of his being than his painterly experience and routine, which is a logical and understandable step. This forest is not a place anyone starts out, there is far too much within a human being that seeks expression and wants out, there is far too much that rattles and clatters, radiates and burns, too much will, too many ambitions, too great a thirst for honour, too much pride and longing and love. This is the place one comes when everything has faded away, this is what the world looks like then, to a painter who can do anything but wants nothing – except to paint.

*

One thing that complicates this line of development in Munch's art and disturbs the idea of a conflict between what is there beforehand and what comes into being through the struggle against it, is the fact that throughout his long life Munch painted certain motifs over and over again. That he returned to *The Sick Child*, returned to *Girls on the Bridge*, returned to *Jealousy*, returned to the scenes in the death chamber, and each time his approach became more technical, less heart-felt. Sometimes he probably did it because he needed the money and these were his most popular pictures, other times it may have been that he had sold the pictures but wanted to have them too. What had once been searching and impulse was now repeated as manner. The feeling or impression he had once sought to capture, and which the initial painting was a response to, a search for, was now not one step away but two. But once in a rare while it could happen that this too released something, that the insight and painterly experience he had acquired brought forth something new in an old motif.

In 1882 and 1883, when he was nineteen years old, he painted three different pictures of his younger brother Andreas as he sat reading. He painted one of them again in 1936, when he was seventy-two, and his brother had been dead for more than forty years. The picture was probably painted as a gift to his brother's daughter, who was then middle-aged. The first picture of Andreas is painted realistically, he is seated in a chair by a window with a book in his hands, reading, one leg is crossed over the other, a wintry sunless light falls almost imperceptibly in through the window and settles softly over his left side, while his right side lies in shadow. He is wearing a blue suit, and much of the painting has to do with the lie of the cloth and how the light plays on it and the room where he is sitting. The curtains, heavy and bourgeois, are a faint green, and the wall in the corner behind the left curtain lies in total shadow except for at the bottom, where something that might be a bed or a table with its flap folded down glows faintly in the murk. Beyond the window an empty grey square is visible, on the other side of it stands a row of blocks of flats; beneath their ochre and mint-green walls lies a white stripe that looks like snow. The blocks of flats are painted more simply and with less sophistication than the interior, they give an impression of something a little naive and clumsy, which can be found elsewhere in the painting too – there is something wrong with the knee in relation to the thigh, as if we were seeing it foreshortened at once from the front and from the side, and the ear which is turned towards the window is a little too red considering what the light and the skin elsewhere seem to indicate, and one hand is more like a log than a hand.

What we see is a picture by a talented young painter who is still inexperienced, and who paints pictures of what he has at hand. There is nothing in this painting of what we associate with Munch, no trace of his distinctiveness in either the motif or its execution.

The version he painted fifty-three years later has kept all the elements – the brother's face looks similar, he is seated in exactly the same position in the same chair, the window is there, the blocks of flats in the background, the curtains and the bed or table in the corner – but the impression it gives, the painting's aura, is radically different. Firstly all the elements have been simplified, they are no longer painted with a sensitive awareness of texture and softness, in saturated and gently graded colours, the way the motif presumably looked to him when he painted it for the first time, but are now presented as painted fields almost entirely independent of each other, since the light and its modulations in colour no longer connect them. The suit, for example, is cut off from all the other elements, it is as if the play of light on it now belongs to it alone – rather like the way shadows and folds in medieval icon paintings are painted independently of the light and the physical space and do not seek to create an illusion of shadows and folds but simply indicate them – and the earlier nuances of grey on the white-painted wall are now represented merely by a couple of coarse, abrupt, greenish brushstrokes, while the windowsill and the window frame above are outlined rather than painted. The curtains are now yellow and red as well as green – this is presumably intended to suggest the light – and the previously deep, impenetrable shadow in the corner is now light and reddish. The block of flats on the other side of the square outside is even more stylised, and the angle is somewhat different, so that it no longer extends the depth of the background, as in the original, but rather cuts it off. The odd perspective at the knee, on the other hand, has been retained, and even the redness of the ear, but in this version it doesn't strike one as a shortcoming: this painting's claim to reality is a different one.

What does it say?

The simplification emphasises the reading boy, the subject is his particular presence. And the moment of the painting is no longer just any moment – which is the impression one gets looking at the first painting, where the brother will soon get up and do something else, the day will pass into evening – what matters is this particular moment, not as a part of time but almost torn from it. The brother's face is painted much more simply; the cheeks are beige while the forehead and the chin are orange, and in a strange way we see him more clearly, in particular just how young he is. But the first thing one notices is the shadow upon his downturned eyes, since it is so prominent through not being integrated with the rest. In the first painting the shadow was a part of the room, here it is not, here it lies over the eyes like a band, and it is difficult not to think that Munch in his painting of this boy has marked him with death.

The nineteen-year-old painter naturally knew nothing of what the future would bring, certainly not in painterly terms; he continued to try things out, to grope his way, to search in the years that followed with an ever surer hand, staying within the same pictorial language, driven by a great and manifest desire for colour and the materiality of colour. The seventy-two-year-old painter, for his part, had most of his life behind him, and he didn't grope around, he knew what he was after.

What was it?

It was not to paint the living, but to make the painted come alive. To him that meant capturing the essential in what he saw. That is what he did when he painted the portrait of his brother over again. The light and the room were not essential, he merely indicated them as expeditiously as he could, nor were the details of his brother's figure and face essential, they too were merely noted. That his brother had once sat there in just that way was essential, and it was the feeling he left behind in the room, a feeling not found in the first portrait, his aura, that Munch painted the second time. And the death awaiting him.

What is strange is that even this last portrait of his brother has something naive about it. The naivety of the first picture has to do with the errors in it, since the errors betray a painter who is not fully in control of his subject matter. We see the painter making an effort without quite succeeding. The later picture is made by an experienced painter in full command of his artistic means. Here the naivety has to do with simplification, it is as if the picture through simplification approaches children's drawings, that there is a remnant of something helpless in it, a remnant of the child in Munch. The radical simplifications of the expressionists usually have none of this about them; in the paintings of Emil Nolde and Oskar Kokoschka, for instance, the simplifications often carry undertones of brutality, force and primitiveness. Munch's pictures are seldom brutal. They are open towards violence but more often towards innocence. This is at once a strength and a weakness of his pictures, they are not sophisticated but so open towards the world that it seems to reveal itself defencelessly, as if it is the world that is unguarded, not the artist.

It is difficult to imagine that Munch could have repainted the picture of his brother in 1936 without thinking back to the time when he made the first version, Kristiania in the 1880s, and of who he was when he lived at home with his father, brother and sisters, cared for by his aunt, his mother's sister. We will never know of course, either whether he thought about that time as he walked around alone at Ekely, in all the rooms that were geared solely towards producing pictures, full of paintings and prints, or what it had been like to be him as a nineteen-year-old, nor is there any reason to wish for this, since the reason we still concern ourselves with this wildly solitary man are his paintings, they were his way of expressing himself, that is what he was doing both at nineteen and at seventy-two, and it is this biography, the one that is visible in his paintings, which is relevant and interesting, not because of their connection to his life, but as something in themselves: life as painted reality.

*

The earliest extant painting by Edvard Munch was made in 1880, when he was sixteen. It depicts Telthusbakken, a hillside street lined with wooden houses in Kristiania, with Gamle Aker church looming above it. The sky is light blue, a few white clouds hover in it, otherwise the picture is dominated by a row of white, yellow and ochre houses, the dark green trees in the churchyard, the greyish wall there, a grassy plain in lighter green in front of the houses. It is a wonderful painting, filled with light, but there is something terribly wrong about the dimensions and the perspective, the houses look like doll's houses, and the church appears almost nearer to the viewer than the houses it lies behind. His next paintings are all of country landscapes, often in muted colours, with a peasant woman in the foreground and birches on one side. Munch had already been drawing for several years; these are exercises in a medium that was new to him, and we must assume that his choice of both motifs and mode of expression was based on the kinds of paintings he had seen until then.

At precisely this time, in the same year, another painter also paints his very first paintings, which are not that unlike Munch's; some of them too depict country landscapes with small figures in the foreground and have the same air of being painting exercises. This was in the Netherlands, the painter was Vincent van Gogh. He was already twenty-seven by then, ten years older than Munch, and only ten years later, when Munch was twenty-seven and just setting out upon his career as a painter, van Gogh committed suicide.

In the autumn of 2015 the two artists were brought together in a large comparative exhibition, and, viewing it, it was easy to think that they were akin to each other and had many points in common, both in style and aesthetics as well as world view and perspective on human life. But actually few artists have been more different in temperament and talent than these two; almost the only thing they shared was the desire to paint and the time in which they painted. Munch was a masterful drawer who gradually perfected his technique. He received lessons from Christian Krohg, and from the very beginning he was surrounded by other technically skilled painters, among whom he stood out. He mastered various styles, there is something eclectic about his paintings prior to 1890, some of them resemble Frits Thaulow's pictures, especially those of Akerselva, Oslo's main river, some of them are close to Krohg's, some of his portraits tend towards the baroque, some of the street scenes tend towards Impressionism. Even after he developed his signature style, such elements occasionally reappear in his paintings. So, in order to paint the way we now think of as typical of Munch, he had to rid himself of what he knew, since knowledge stood between him and what he painted, a process which Stian Grøgaard in his book about Munch terms 'unlearning'. Things stood very differently, almost diametrically opposed, in the case of van Gogh, who must be the least eclectic painter the world has ever seen, in the sense that the correspondence between what he had in him and what he painted was so great. It is as if nothing stood between him and his pictures. No unlearning, just a continual process of learning, in a life's work which is strikingly consistent and which at least in retrospect seems to move towards something it eventually attains, in the explosions of light and colour which dominate his very last paintings.

Van Gogh's early paintings are dark, brownish, earth-bound, lumpen, heavy. He paints still lifes of potatoes! Then gradually they change, it is as if they gain in colour, gain in light, and as if only then do they realise that light exists and want more and more of it, more light, more colour, until they end up drunk on beauty and life's intensity.

I never understood the force that light possesses in van Gogh's pictures until I saw the originals in the museum in Amsterdam, for the reproductions are unable to render it, since the light isn't graduated and modulated in the motif but belongs to the colours, their physicality.

As incredible as it may seem, all those pictures, that whole universe, were produced in the course of ten years. Munch, who as we have seen began to paint in the same year as van Gogh, spent the same period exploring the medium, in paintings that are infinitely more cool and controlled, still marked by the naturalism then dominant in Norway, and he was concerned with technical issues, as for example in *Morning* from 1884, which was one of the first paintings he exhibited.

To his friend Olav Paulsen, he writes this about the painting:

> I am at work on a 'girl'. Yes I suppose you find it odd that once again I am at it with a girl in a morning mood but the motif was far too beautiful for me not to make use of it. It is quite simply a girl who is rising from her chaste repose and, seated on the edge of her bed, pulling on her stockings – The bed is whitish and in addition there are white sheets, a white nightgown, a bedside table with a white cover, white curtains and a

blue wall. That is the colour effect. I don't know whether I will be able to pull it off since it is very difficult, but I hope it will work.[2]

And it did work, all that white really does give a chaste impression, as he wanted it to, at the same time that he managed to give life to the white, depth to the room and volume and weight to the woman's body. It is a beautiful painting, and it was made by a twenty-year-old who, like the eighteen-year-old, must have desired the materiality of colour more than that of reality, or at least must have valued them equally; the blue wall against all that white, the beauty of it, is what brings this painting to life.

The same desire is evident in another picture he painted that year, *The Infirmary at Helgelandsmoen*, with its blue-green firewall against the reddish slanted ceiling and wooden wall, colours which almost completely neutralise the presence of the three people in the room, or make it secondary. The painting lives in its colours, it is the wall and the firewall the painter has invested himself in, not in the human figures.

In some sense, all of Munch's pictures from this period are exercises, not necessarily because they are unfinished, but because they are either responses to technical challenges, explorations of new territory or self-infatuated, and therefore not enough in themselves to stand alone. The first picture which does, the first painting by Munch to present itself in its own right, is in my view another one that he painted as a twenty-year-old, *Inger Munch in Black*.

It is a simple half-length portrait of his sister Inger, wearing a black dress against a black background, her hands down by her sides, her gaze turned slightly to the left. She is sixteen years old and she has dressed up in her confirmation dress, which alone sets the mood of the picture, the joining of youthfulness with solemnity.

This painting too is unfinished, there is something sketchy about the hands, and a rather unmotivated or poorly defined field of red in the lower right-hand corner, while at the same time the left arm is indistinctly painted, but the air of incompleteness no longer feels like a shortcoming, since the person portrayed has such a powerful presence, a presence which does away with everything else. She is all that matters. Not how she is painted, not how the volume of head and torso have been rendered, but who she is, standing there. In this painting it is as if Munch himself has stepped back a little, let go of his own self in order to make room for hers, and I can't help thinking it must mean something that this happened when he painted a motif that was close to him, a motif from his own life. Only then did the sensitivity he possessed become free enough to find expression. Something in this motif was more important than the technical challenges of the painting and relegated the painterly issues to the background, while at the same time it was only then that his painting really began. This ability, to both step aside for the motif, make room for it, see it and sense it, which demands a great openness to the world, and at the same time be able to bring out one's own vision in a painting, is perhaps the decisive quality for every artist. Therein lay van Gogh's genius, in his total self-effacement when he painted, entirely faithful to what he saw, which paradoxically became filled with himself. Self-effacement, isn't that too a kind of responsiveness? That one's pitch is perfect because there is no self there to correct it? Munch had to bridge a greater

distance between his eye and his hand, there is rarely anything ecstatic about his paintings, almost always something
calculated. I think that is why he eventually began to paint
so rapidly, why so often there was something sketch-like
about his pictures, because he was trying to get to the picture before thought did. About this he himself wrote, 'I act
either precipitously and with Inspiration hastily (thought-
lessly and unhappily – and with Inspiration and happy
effect) or with long Deliberation – and anxiously – the Result
is then often weaker and can be a failure – the Result can
become the work's Undoing.'[3]

I think that was also why as a young man he began to
paint closer to his own experiences and his own life, in
which emotion balanced calculation and might even erase it,
and the relation between what he had within him and what
he painted became more immediate.

Inger Munch in Black has been one of my favourite pictures since the first time I saw it, yet I have never been able
to pinpoint exactly what it is that makes it so appealing.
Whatever the painting communicates, it does so silently and
wordlessly, and what I understand it with is similarly silent
and wordless. Can one then speak of 'understanding' at all?
Yes, for intuitive knowledge exists, silent wisdom exists,
instinctive insight exists, and I believe this unarticulated
understanding of the world comprises a much larger part of
our self than we usually imagine. Precisely that it is based
on intuitions and sensations, never explicitly formulated or
argued for, allows it to evade the apparatus with which we
usually comprehend the world, reason and the language of
reason, and in this way remain almost invisible and
unacknowledged.

To write about a painting deepens the same problem. A painting addresses itself directly to the emotions, and when the emotions are explained and words assigned to what is wordless, it becomes something else. It doesn't help, somehow, to point to the picture's use of diagonals, how the lines of the two white hands amid all that blackness lead one's attention to the face, which is the centre of the picture, since this only says something about how the painting works but nothing about what kind of effect we are dealing with.

There is little to indicate that Munch was a good judge of human nature, he seems to have been too full of himself to understand others, but this portrait isn't an analysis of his sister, it is a sensing of her. It is filled with the emotions that her presence evokes, so if anything he was a feeler of human nature. One who sensed souls, sensed objects and landscapes. If someone had asked Munch to say who his sister was, or if he had written down what he thought of her personality, what he said or wrote might have given us a vague idea of her, but her uniqueness, what made Inger Inger, would escape us. It doesn't in this painting, we see at once who she is, and it is this presence that is the subject of the picture.

I am filled with something resembling happiness when I look at it. Something unconditionally good.

Why?

I think it has to do with dignity. And thereby with hope. The skin beside her left eye, where it meets the cheekbone, is accentuated with bright light, one's attention is involuntarily drawn to it, towards that field, which darkens into a shadow beneath the eye. While her gaze seems remote, with a hint of pride in it, the skin below it is faintly reddish, and this colours her gaze, it is as if she had just now been crying. The wholly black background creates a sense that she has come from something, that she is piercing something, and the black confirmation dress ties her closely to it, as if she is still in it and looking out from it. In that gaze, looking out from grief but still not free of it, there is pride, it is as if her gaze says that this grief is not me, it is merely something that has befallen me. There is no struggle in the painting, no conflict in her eyes, but acceptance. These are the conditions of my life. Hence the dignity, and hence hope. It also has to do with being young, when one's feeling of being alive is at its most intense and has an existence of its own wholly independent of whatever else might happen in one's life. It is as if the twenty-year-old Munch has managed to capture precisely this in his portrait of his sister, what she is and what the conditions of her life are, that which binds and that which sets one free. I doubt this is something he thought about or reflected upon, he would have been too young. But emotions are ageless, they connect us directly to the world, and it is through emotion that he has approached his sister's presence and 'understood' it.

Whether he himself felt that he had come closer to something essential, something truer when he painted the portrait of Inger, I obviously don't know, but he clearly did when he began to paint *The Sick Child* the following year, in 1885, taking as his starting point the memory he had of his sister's sickbed and death, and in which for the first time he sought a way to express his inner world of feelings and sensations pictorially, and by doing so, alone among the young painters in Kristiania during the 1880s and 1890s, he broke radically with the prevailing artistic idiom.

The Sick Child was like a feeler, a venture out into the unknown, the painting was mocked, ridiculed and reviled, and in the next few years it was as if he fell back to something safer, at the same time as he was learning, until his pictorial world exploded at the beginning of the 1890s, and the pictures we primarily associate with him were painted in an unprecedented burst of force and radicality.

If one is to compare him to anyone else from that time, no painters seem relevant, but rather an author, namely Knut Hamsun. They were of the same generation, Hamsun was born four years before Munch, in 1859, and his first novel, *Hunger* (1890), came to define the literary decade of the 1890s in Norway in a way similar to how Munch's pictures from that decade did in the world of painting. Before *Hunger* literary realism dominated, with novels such as Alexander Kielland's *Garman & Worse*, where the whole of society was depicted through myriad characters in a densified drama where the individual characters' psychologies, which were woven together with the social class they belonged to, decided their fate, whether they would rise or sink or remain in their place. Balance was decisive, it ensured that not even the most irrational act or character disrupted the whole but instead conformed with the greater picture, which seemed to moderate everything human. That is how Gustave Flaubert's *Madame Bovary* is narrated too. The space in which the story unfolds is as important as the story. This space does not perish when Emma Bovary perishes – the space is the place, understood both geographically, culturally and existentially, in which the story unfolds, and it is fundamentally stable.

Hunger disrupts this space with a radicality that even now, 130 years after it was written, is startling. Not only is perspective situated within one person who sees the world from his point of view – first-person novels of course existed then as now – but that perspective itself is the novel's main concern: it is about the place from which the world is viewed. There is no plot, no construction of characters, everything centres on the person seeing, and thereby more on the way he sees it than on what is seen. The effect is great even today, for it is as if Hamsun through this describes the world as it comes into being, as it arises for the main protagonist, from the weather on the day he wakes up in his place of shelter to the things he sees and the people he encounters. The world is in the present tense, the world is here and now, and this renders a plot wholly superfluous, for anything at all can happen! We live in this excitement every day, for in our lives too anything can happen. The expectations we have, based on recognition and prior knowledge, remove the excitement from daily life rather in the same way that plot structure and the construction of characters can do in classic novels and films. We are not exposed, we are safe, we live in a secure and predictable space. The novel and the film look after us.

Hamsun's protagonist is starving, he has no money, he lives from hand to mouth, but it isn't this which creates the intense presence or destabilises the space of the novel, it is the way the novel is narrated, the inner perspective, how the external action is steeped in the emotions and thoughts it evokes, or even that what happens, happens *in* the emotions and thoughts, before our very eyes. In *Hunger* the world is the world of the starving protagonist; when he dies, it dies with him.

Hamsun found a new literary space, one which came into being as he wrote, and perhaps the most striking thing about it is that both the past and the future are practically non-existent. This makes the space unpredictable and as if quivering, like a flickering image on a TV screen in the second before it stabilises and becomes sharp and clear, which happens every time the protagonist leaves the room and enters a new one.

Edvard Munch grew up in the same culture as Hamsun, they must have been imbued with the same values and exposed to similar influences, and realism and naturalism in painting, which is what Munch primarily related to, was not unlike the realism prevalent in literature. Erik Werenskiold's painting *Peasant Burial* from 1883, Eilif Peterssen's *Mother Utne* from 1888 and Christian Krohg's *Albertine at the Police Doctor's Waiting Room* from 1886 were all painted while Munch was a young man, and in different ways represented the prevailing norm for what a painting was supposed to portray and how it was supposed to look. Death, poverty, ageing, sex and prostitution were the themes of the day, all of them viewed from a distance in spaces so stable that they are not threatened by what they contain. For Krohg this was presumably a concrete issue, like Kielland he was a socially conscious man from the bourgeoisie, indignant about poverty and injustice, and if he was able to identify with the conditions under which Albertine the prostitute lived, he couldn't communicate it in his painting except through a considerable distance, which the space and the rules of art maintained. One could look at destitution, suffering, poverty and sexuality only if one's gaze was not itself part of what is seen, but external to it. We follow the same principle today: to feel compassion for what we see is fine, the most extreme misery, sex and death are fine, but only within a system that doesn't bring us too close to it or make us a part of it.

No art is free of morals, for the simple reason that all art entails a set of assessments of reality, and they are always social in nature, since no such thing as non-social art has ever existed, but – and this is important – art is moral first and foremost through form, since it is form which establishes a relation between the viewer and the viewed. Considered in this way, *Hunger* is a more significant moral work than *Garman & Worse*, although the latter expresses a set of high-minded humanist opinions while in *Hunger* there isn't a single sentence that can be cited in support of anything either high-minded or humanistic.

This is really about truth, which I believe to be both unchanging and at the core of all art. I think the essential thing about truth is that it must be experienced, and in order for it to be experienced, I think it has to appear nakedly, not woven into inherited notions. The driving force for all art is to find an expression that is true, and if you are a twenty-four-year-old painter in Kristiania in 1888, you notice if the set of painterly methods at your disposal is inadequate, you notice if you feel blocked; and if this is not a part of a conscious process of thought – it rarely is, truth is something one senses intuitively, and artistic work occurs through intuition – it still presents the young artist with two choices: either strangle the sense of inadequacy at birth and find the paintings satisfactory even though they are distant from the impulse which compelled them into being, or scrape, paint, scrape, paint, discard, start afresh, seek, search, paint, scrape, until the painting 'answers' and a kind of unity or congruence arises between the driving force and the result. Perhaps this never happens, perhaps it happens after ten years, perhaps it happens after ten days.

Munch's *The Scream* relates to Krohg's *Albertine at the Police Doctor's Waiting Room* in much the same way *Hunger* relates to *Garman & Worse*. In *The Scream* the world is not a stable space in which an event unfolds. The event in itself is neither notable nor scandalous, there is no prostitute about to be examined for venereal disease by the police surgeon, but a person with an open mouth standing by a railing on a height above a city, covering his ears. What is shocking about the picture, and what was considered scandalous when it was exhibited for the first time, is that the entire space is subsumed into the face and the state of mind it expresses. The space is recognisable, it is Oslo with the Oslo fjord, probably seen from the ridge of Ekebergåsen, but it is greatly distorted, the cityscape has been reduced to some undulating blueish strokes, the fjord is a few yellow lines, the sky powerful waves of red and orange. If one looks first at one of the realistic paintings from the 1880s and then at this picture, it is difficult to believe that they belong to the same time and culture, *The Scream* looks like something from a different world. But all that has happened is what happened in *Hunger*, the perspective has been moved into a single person, and the work's main concern is the place from which the world is viewed, reality as experienced by this single individual *is* the world. Everything seen is coloured by emotions and moods, which are continually changing. But what makes Munch's painting so powerful and strikingly effective is that it leaves the viewer defenceless. The emotions it expresses are transferred instantly and with full force. This defencelessness arises precisely through there being no space to lessen the force of the scream, that there is no before or after, the now fills everything we see.

Space – both the geographical and the temporal – is reconciliatory, since it guarantees perspectives of continuity and alternative courses of development. But in *The Scream* the space is closed, we cannot escape what is happening in the picture, there is no distance to be had. This must have been the most provocative thing about Munch's paintings from this time: that the distance which the prevailing pictorial idiom entailed and which made it possible to relate not only to disease, prostitution and death in public without involving oneself or one's own life, but also to the sublime, the beautiful and the exalted, this distance was no longer there. The distance to the painted was suspended too – in *The Scream* the brushstrokes are visible, and the painting is sketchy, it has an unfinished air, not least the broad reddish-purple line running down along the entire right edge of the picture. In any other picture it would have broken the illusion, but *The Scream* is painted so wildly that it intensifies instead. Imagine what such a broad, closed brushstroke would have done to the precisely painted and realistic paintings from the same time, for instance Werenskiold's beautiful paintings from the Setesdalen valley – their entire magic, which lies in the credibility of the pictorial space, would have been ruined.

The titles *Hunger* and *The Scream* resemble each other, both are short, almost primitively simple, both denote something bodily, something that expresses itself before words, something primary and almost pre-human, in the sense that the wordless scream and hunger are also animal. They also share the thing that was new about them at the time of their creation, namely their extreme subjectivity, the reality of the single individual. And both totally destroy, or completely ignore, the stable, collective space. They entailed a new art, a new space, a new time.

But they did this 130 years ago, so the crucial question is perhaps why they still seem relevant, why they remain such a living part of the culture. As I write this book about Munch, relating so directly to his pictures, it is as if a writer of Munch's time were to write about a Norwegian painter from the 1760s and relate to his paintings and the history of their creation as if they were still relevant. Which I suppose quite simply means that the new era which Munch's pictures heralded and were a part of is still the era in which we live.

*

It is ice cold in the room where I am writing this, the heat pump has stopped working while at the same time the outside temperature has fallen sharply, and the small wood-burning stove is only able to heat the air within a one-metre range, no matter how much wood I feed it. So I am sitting here dressed in a heavy outer jacket, wool hat, scarf and boots. Yet it doesn't look like winter outside, the temperature is just above zero and the lawn is still green with streaks of yellow, here and there almost covered with leaves, which autumn and the first month of winter have turned mostly dark brown and reddish brown, still not rotten but heavy and wet. Beyond the lawn the boards of the house wall shine red against the whitewashed foundation wall.

In such a world, so full of colours playing against each

other and appearing in new ways every day, sometimes unfathomably beautiful, full of mysteries one can ponder for a lifetime, one might ask what we need art for. Art is of course itself a part of the world, like everything we make, but art distinguishes itself from objects by always being more than them, in that besides being an object in reality, it also creates a reality of its own, next to or beyond the one we usually see and inhabit.

What kind of a phenomenon is that? And of what use is it to us?

At the end of November I visited an exhibition in London of the work of the German artist Anselm Kiefer. The title of the show was *Walhalla,* and it comprised various objects, installations and paintings. It opened with a long corridor full of beds, as in a hospital ward or an army camp. The beds were made of lead, so were the duvets and pillows, but despite the resulting colossal weight, all the little crinkles, folds and imprints left by the moulds created a sense of lightness and careless chance, like the impression a recently abandoned bed can give, while at the same time the weight and immobility of the material fixed the lightness of that moment in something else, something immutable – in a place without time. And where are we then? Time is the space in which our lives unfold, life is one long continuous movement, it never comes to rest, never pauses. Even when we sleep, our eyes move beneath our eyelids, our ribcage rises and falls, our heart beats and thumps, our blood trickles and gurgles, and even while we are sitting still on the sofa, exhausted by the day's work, our thoughts glide through our consciousness, never the same, never identical, as our days are never the same, never identical. We cannot escape time, it is a fundamental condition of our existence, and we are therefore excluded from non-time, from timelessness – it doesn't exist for us. We may be able to see it, or to imagine it, but only as something on the other side of an abyss. The leaden beds in the London gallery were outside of time in the sense that the moment they represented, through the folds and irregularities in the material, would never be succeeded by another moment, but would remain thus, unchanging, for all time. A human being in a bed is moreover a vulnerable human being; I am thinking of my youngest daughter as I write this, she is three years old, and every morning I lift her out of her cot and into the day, where she takes up everything from the previous day in a continuity which must never ever be broken – but if it is, that is what I will see, the imprint of her movements on the sheet and the duvet. It was imprints such as these, of absent bodies, that Kiefer's lead intensified, and it did something to the sense of time; these beds had not been abandoned just now, this very instant, they had just been abandoned a long, long time ago, and perhaps, it struck me as I walked alongside them, they had belonged to gods or heroes.

A room opened to the left, in the middle stood a huge spiral staircase from which hung shirts and dresses. These were the Valkyries, who in Norse mythology chose the warriors who would die on the battlefield. A little further on, the main gallery opened up, in it hung several enormous paintings of towers rearing up from a desert-yellow expanse, in one of them what looked like columns of smoke were rising.

Only a few days earlier I had been sent some photographs by Paolo Pellegrin, who had accompanied Kurdish forces through Syria towards Aleppo. In these photos too enormous columns of smoke rose from a flat and sandy landscape, and it was impossible not to link Kiefer's paintings to the photos, while at the same time the paintings also opened on to a world of myth, that of the Tower of Babel and the destruction of Sodom and Gomorrah.

Apart from a photograph of Kiefer himself there wasn't a single image or representation of a human being in the entire exhibition, it consisted exclusively of beds and bed-clothes, spiral staircase and shirts and dresses, desiccated trees and rocks, and paintings of desert landscapes empty of people. A bed and a spiral staircase are articles of daily use, so are shirts and dresses, they belong to the everyday and aren't loaded with much of anything – nor are desert landscapes or trees and rocks. But here, juxtaposed in this way in this gallery, they almost collapsed under the weight of significance.

Where was the significance? The objects and the paintings pointed to it or opened a space where it could appear. But where was it before it was invoked?

Myths are precisely timeless, they are not tied to a specific moment but concern that about us or within us which never changes. They are set in motion at a specific time, but as soon as the exhibition ends or the book is closed, they again disappear out of time. All works of art open up such spaces, they knock down a wall where we are standing and cause another reality to emerge. What they open on to are not necessarily old myths or archetypal notions of course, but – and this is an essential feature of art – over time they themselves come to resemble myths, since an artwork in itself is unchanging, outside time. An artist paints a portrait of a person, twenty years pass and the artist dies, thirty years pass and the person in the portrait dies, three hundred years pass and we see the painting in a museum in Madrid. What we see is a moment in time, the moment when a particular artist applied particular brushstrokes of paint in a particular room. Everything else has changed and disappeared with time, but not the painting. When we stand in front of it, we realise its significance, we bring it to life, we draw it into our own time and our own reality. Art works with the living, it attempts to grasp life in time, as it is in precisely this moment, and when it succeeds, life in time becomes timeless.

Kiefer approached it from the opposite direction, he sought to grasp the timeless, to install it here among us, and the effect this had, at least on me when I saw the exhibition, was to render current events in the world, in particular violent and destructive events such as the ongoing war in Syria and the unceasing terror in Iraq, suddenly no longer just a distant and irrelevant flickering in which people were no more than numbers, eighty dead here, five hundred dead there, but present. This was achieved through Kiefer's often criticised monumentality, because it makes death so vast and history so deep, and thereby life so fragile and irreplaceable, not just mine, not just yours, but everybody's.

That is how myths function. They deal with a few people placed in a few situations – think of Hector and Achilles in the *Iliad*, or Cain and Abel in the Bible – who are given such exceptional weight that, several thousand years after the stories about them were told for the first time, they are still present in culture. A fratricide that occurs now, say in Malmö, will go unnoticed, the local newspaper might devote a few lines to it, but for everyone not directly related to the brothers it won't mean anything, it won't leave an impression, it will be almost as if nothing had happened. Or take any single event in a war, a soldier killed with a knife, a corpse dragged behind a jeep, it will vanish from the world in the same way for everyone except those directly concerned. But if one hears about the fratricide while thinking of Cain and Abel, or about acts of war with the *Iliad* in mind, one comes to understand that all events carry the same weight, that everything that happens between people is equally significant. One also comes to understand that everything has happened before, that being human was the same five thousand years ago as it is today. Myths are communal experiences, and what they do is give our lives a space other than that of time in which to unfold. Myths have no existence in themselves, they have no place of their own, but they enter the world every time they are activated, as in the Kiefer exhibition in London.

Art resembles myth in the sense that it gives individual people and single events the same exceptional weight, and in a similar way places them in a space beyond time – think for example of the scene in *The Godfather II* where Michael Corleone arranges for his older brother to be killed, how many emotions converge on that particular point, and how simply the extremely complicated relationship between brothers is represented yet without diminishing its complexity and emotional depth. Or think of Edvard Munch's *The Sick Child*, the mild gaze of the dying girl, full of concern for the grieving woman who is sitting beside her. Or think of Maggie Nelson's novel *The Argonauts*, in which the birth towards the end is described as if it were happening for the very first time in the world. And so it is for the woman giving birth, and through her description of it, for us reading about it. I have never ordered the killing of my brother, I have never lost a sister, and I have never given birth to a child. But because of that movie, that painting and that book I have been present in those spaces, and those spaces are a part of my experience as a human being. It might not be important in itself, but it is important because it tells us that every moment is really like that, that every relation is really like that, something in itself, with a significance of its own, which must be acknowledged and given space to exist within us.

The heavy unchanging lead, the light and arbitrary imprints we leave, the inviolability of life, the inescapable nothingness of death. These are entities we all know and sometimes stop to consider, but to confront us with them, letting us be filled with them and making us understand them through our feelings is something only art can do. Munch closed up space to make it more acute, in *The Scream* the only thing that matters is the feeling of the moment, while Kiefer opens space up to link the acute and the immediate with history and in that way gives it depth, not least because the sheer mass of suffering continually being conveyed in our media-dominated age has turned the acute into a permanent state and thereby almost eradicated it as experience. The time lag between an event in the world and our awareness of it has become so short that it is as if we are living in the instantaneous world of *The Scream*, and the demands of art have therefore become the opposite of those which Munch set himself; time must now be given a new place in space.

*

A week after I saw the exhibition, I met Anselm Kiefer in person, in his studio outside Paris. I went there to interview him and to watch while he worked. The studio had once been a department store warehouse, it was gigantic, both Kiefer and his assistants used bicycles to get around. He lived there, at one end a separate floor had been built with three large rooms where he painted, plus a library, several living rooms and a kitchen. He worked every day all year round, it was a way of life, and although he was seventy-two and I had turned forty-eight the previous day, after eight hours of watching him work I was exhausted, while he was still in full swing when I left. The hall, much larger than a football field, was filled with pictures and installations he had made. The only other artist whose pictures I saw there, in Kiefer's strange and in its separation from outside reality almost sub-aquatic world, was Edvard Munch. In the library, on the sides of some of the bookcases, hung Munch's woodcut *Towards the Forest* and a couple of other pictures I immediately recognised, including the one of a man and a woman who seem to hover about each other in outer space.

It seemed a little odd, for Kiefer's and Munch's art are strikingly different in appearance. Kiefer's theme is myth, history, time and destruction, death and annihilation, but also destruction as a new beginning, and a notable feature of his art, at least at first glance, is that he himself is not present in it. Few would call Kiefer's art personal. While Munch painted his personal traumas in a symbolistic expressionism where the outer was only there to give form to or illustrate the inner, and where the historical or the social was almost entirely absent.

I asked Kiefer about his relationship to Munch, he more or less dismissed the question with an impatient gesture of his head while saying that Munch was a good graphic artist. I have heard several artists say the same thing, that Munch's greatest achievement was as a graphic artist, and that his real talent lay in the line. That Kiefer felt a connection to that part of Munch's art isn't so strange, and that precisely *Towards the Forest* hung in his library makes sense – Kiefer's art is full of trees and forests, throughout his artistic career he has returned to that motif. One of his masterpieces, *Varus*, depicts woods covered in snow, with bloodspots and the names of German romantics written across the canvas – it is the battle between the Teutons and the Romans in the Teutoburger Forest, it is the Nazis' use of the historical event and of the forest as a myth of origin and claim to authenticity, it is the woods surrounding the extermination camps, but it is also Kiefer's own childhood and youth in the Black Forest and the significance of trees in religion, the tree of life, the tree of knowledge, the world tree Yggdrasil. Another, never-exhibited work of art I saw there consists of boxes with cut-out trees as if on a stage, with photographs from his personal life dangling from them, of the first ball he attended, of an aunt who died young, of close friends. Kiefer has said that our stories begin in the forest, and it is this kind of forest Munch depicted, a dark jagged field towards which a man and a woman are walking, closely entwined. We see them from behind as they head towards the forest, there is something infinitely fragile and vulnerable about them, it is as if they are supporting each other, holding each other up. Man and woman entwined is of course a familiar Munch motif, with the woman as vampire sucking the blood and life out of the man. Here the relationship is one of equality, yet not uncomplicated, in one version

59

of the motif the woman is naked while the man is fully clothed, as if unable ever to come quite near her.

The forest, what is that? Freedom? Yes, but freedom as disappearance, freedom as death. The figures are oddly clumsily drawn, almost as if by a child, but the picture has a roughness about it, something unrefined and wild, which contrasts with the clumsiness and turns it into something tender and frail. So much longing on such a small surface. And so much force, so much of the forest comes to expression here, in that the texture of the woodblock on which the image is carved and then pressed against paper is so visible. This is something Munch sought to get closer to in his art, the material aspect of the pictures he made, and something similar is found in Kiefer, who goes one step further and incorporates materials such as ashes, straw, sand and bits of wood directly into his pictures, and lets the arbitrary patterns and forms taken by poured molten lead form part of the picture. That for Munch the picture was also an object in itself, independent of what it represented, in other words its material and physical aspect, became especially clear during the final phase of his life, when he exposed his pictures to the elements and in that way let them be marked by nature – which was also part of the carelessness which characterised his relationship to his own pictures, that he painted quickly and often failed to complete his paintings, leaving them sketchy and unfinished.

Later Kiefer said that he had Munch's *catalogue raisonné* and that he had been surprised the first time he looked through all the paintings, since so many of them, perhaps close to 70 per cent, were weak. He moderated his stance at once, saying that those paintings were more of a process, they were on their way somewhere, in contrast to the finished ones, the good ones, the masterpieces.

Kiefer also said that his assistant had been instructed to destroy certain of his works if he were to die suddenly, pieces that were unfinished or second-rate.

This made an impression on me, perhaps since I was unable to evaluate his pictures myself, all of them were so highly Kieferesque, so closely related to each other. Munch had evidently thought differently, in his will he left all of his pictures, the whole lot, to the Municipality of Oslo, and it is impossible to know how he viewed his own paintings, what in his eyes were failures, unfinished, what was below par, and what he was pleased with. Based on what I know about him, I think he didn't really care, at least not during the final phase of his life, when he simply painted.

When I watched Kiefer work on that day in December and saw him pouring molten lead over an exceptionally beautiful painting of a snow-covered forest landscape, I asked him if he wasn't afraid of ruining the pictures, whether he ever felt he should have stopped the process earlier. He laughed and said that all artists are iconoclasts.

*

Two kilometres from where I am sitting and writing this, a British photographer has his studio. His name is Stephen Gill, and I was just up there visiting him, he wanted to show me what he has been working on for the last three years. Although Glemmingebro is a small village with around 300 inhabitants, I had met him just a couple of times before, at the kindergarten where we both had children and at a new year's party. I knew that before he moved here he had lived and worked in London. I had been meaning to contact him for a long time, I don't know very many people in this area with whom one can talk about art and pictures, at least not on his level, but I hadn't figured out how to, I'm not very social and it is not in my nature to simply call someone. So I was happy when he called. He had sent me a text message with instructions on how to get there – drive up onto the low plain just outside the village, turn off on the gravel road at the end of it, after a kilometre the house would be on the right.

I drove for several kilometres inland without seeing any house that fitted the description, turned round in a driveway and drove back the way I had come. The fields stretched as far as I could see in every direction, pale yellow, winter green, wet brown. The sky was white, as it had been for several days. I had never driven this way before, and that alone, to find myself beyond the place I usually drove past, changed the landscape or gave me a different impression of it. It was as if the landscape belonged to the road and was laid out in particular fields and angles which my new position suddenly suspended, so that the feeling of plains, of kilometre-long flat fields, was resurrected in me as I sat behind the wheel peering in every direction as I drove slowly along.

It is often windy here, the great sails of wind that build up over the ocean meet no obstacles and come rushing in over the land, but today it was perfectly still, the light stood motionless in the air, and all the muted colours unfolded calmly in it.

Usually I don't notice the light when it is as neutral as it was now, and I am nearly always busy with something at this time of day, so the sight of it while I was out of my usual setting reminded me of other mornings elsewhere, especially some mornings in Bergen when I had come home from a night shift and sat for a while in the apartment before going to bed, the light over Danmarksplass could be as calm and neutral as it was here now, when the jumble of cars, people and buildings didn't suck me in but left me in peace.

A dark-clad figure stood outside one of the houses holding a cup. As I approached I saw that it was Stephen. I rolled down the window and asked where I could park.

– Anywhere you like, he said.

There were several buildings on the property, all of them slightly decayed.

– I'm so glad you could come, he said when I had parked and climbed out of the car.

– Good to see you, I said.

We went into a room that looked like a workshop and up the stairs to his studio on the first floor. It was large and open, with a ceiling several metres high. Bookcases full of photography books ran along the lower part of the walls, a huge table covered with books and photographs stood in the middle of the room, on the floor to the right of the table a large number of photos were laid out.

– Sit down, he said and pulled out a chair from a bench in front of the window.

– Would you like some coffee?

– Yes, please, I said, sitting down.

– Go ahead and smoke, if you want, he said. – I might have one myself.

His eyes were brown and warm, his body language eager. He was conspicuously kind, it was as if I was being enveloped in attentiveness, at the same time he talked continuously. He told me he had worked constantly when he was living in

London, every day, completely absorbed in his projects, and that eventually he had had a breakdown. That's when he had moved here, with his wife Lena and their two children. He also told me that he was unable to filter out information, it was a condition that had only been diagnosed relatively recently, until then he had thought it was like that for everybody. He explained it by giving an example. If he was withdrawing money from a cashpoint, he said, he wouldn't be paying attention only to the text appearing on the screen, but to everything that was going on and being said in the vicinity. Everything was given the same weight, he was bombarded with information, relevant and irrelevant side by side, which he now believed he had used photography as a way of containing.

– In one of my books I tried to tone down all the information, to take mute and slow photos, that was in Japan, wait, let me show you . . .

He brought out a book and handed it to me. The title was *Coming Up For Air*. The photographs were truly muted, the colours were soft and the boundaries between them diffuse. There was something sub-aquatic about them, also in actual fact, for some of them depicted creatures in aquariums, and the gliding nebulousness that surrounded them was carried out into the streets of Tokyo, there was a pale pink umbrella, a light blue jacket, a gentle stream of people, a reddish seahorse suspended in the water.

The photos were beautiful but also unsettling because the beauty came from a world that was depicted accurately yet still wasn't realistic, wasn't the way things looked to me. It was like seeing images from someone else's dream of Japan. Or perhaps images of how a deaf person would experience the country. Muted, soundless, colours floating around in the streets.

– But that's not what I really wanted to show you, he said. – I've been working on a project ever since we moved here, and I think it's finished now. Would you like to have a look?

– Please, I said and was handed a large book with original photographs. They were exclusively photos from the area, taken within a radius of maybe ten kilometres, all of them pictures of nature. They offered no overview, had neither horizon nor sky, just dense forest spaces and motifs photographed at such close range that they often dissolved into patterns and surfaces, establishing striking correspondences between snails, stones, bark and the pelt of a wild boar, between antlers and branches, or between a stag's legs and tree trunks, between leaves and currents in water, between currents in water and snails, stones, bark and the pelt of a wild boar. There were night-time photos of animals and birds, photographed with no human presence, so that a feeling that they had been seen as they were when they were by themselves arose and in a way spread to the other pictures, which thereby not only revealed a secret and hidden world – for I live here and have seen this landscape every day for more than six years without ever realising that this too existed here – but also opened it out towards the past and the future, that is as it was before we arrived and as it will be after we have gone.

A world of its own, complete in itself, independent of us, that is what he had depicted. But it wasn't unaffected by us of course – one can imagine hikers barging in on the scene, loggers operating chainsaws, cars droning past on the roads, helicopters and planes whizzing over the trees. Humans were present but did not participate, they were like shadows from a shadow world, a noise, a rush.

This independence from us of course applies to all things, even those that are closest to us, but it is almost impossible to perceive and thereby acknowledge, since as soon as we see something, we filter it through our experience and understanding and in that way make it our own, a part of ourselves. Stephen's photos re-established the distance to things by moving so close to them, and by upending our visual hierarchy, by circumventing the centre we automatically establish when we look at something.

The world devoid of humans, the separate reality of things, this is what the Norwegian author Tor Ulven so often wrote about. That I saw Ulven in these photographs may mean either that Stephen and Ulven were seeking the same thing, or that Ulven has influenced my view of art and nature so deeply that it was his gaze I saw and his thoughts I was thinking as I stood looking at Stephen's pictures. For that is an essential feature of all significant art, it not only shows us something but simultaneously teaches us to see what it shows us elsewhere and in other objects and phenomena.

Although photography is different from painting, and to an even greater degree from literature, the problems it raises are essentially the same. How form determines what can be shown or said. Stephen talked about how classic photography selects what is important, how it makes something central, and the coercion this entails. And how the photographer himself so easily comes to occupy a place in the photo, through its composition, at the same time that composition is an unavoidable element of the picture. I realised that nearly everything he did had to do with getting away from this. He sought to get away from the centre, away from himself, and he sought out the accidental, processes he couldn't control. He had buried a series of photographs of an area of east London and left them in the ground for a few days; what happened to them became a part of the physical photographs and connected them to the place in a very different and more concrete way than the light did. In another series he had filled the camera body with dust and debris from the place he was working, including ants, and these appeared as shadows in the resulting photos. A third series was taken by a pond, and as with the forest photos there were none that provided an overview, merely parts and fragments. Some of the parts were microscopic, of life within drops of water, others were of people who lived by the pond, they were blurred and dim, for he shot the photos with the lens covered in water from the same pond. From a book entitled *Archaeology in Reverse* he showed me photos of things which still haven't come into being, the motifs are from one of those peripheral parts of London where nature, industry and the streets lie side by side, and which in themselves seem unfinished or indeterminate but which Stephen has opened up still further by focusing on concrete objects or events which aren't objects or events in themselves but on their way to becoming so. Another book he showed me was made by a Russian artist, it was really an exhibition catalogue, and it showed pictures of objects being used for something other than what they were originally intended for. Forks which have been turned into an antenna, a fur which has become a hat, a metal pipe which has become a toy pistol.

It was as if what I had been reflecting on these last few years with regard to art and literature had suddenly been made visible, as if that was what Stephen was showing me. For where something doesn't yet exist but is coming into being, that is the essential place in all creation, that is where you have to get to, and the job consists as much of getting there as of the actual work done once you are there. And one thing becoming another, transformation, that is art's method. The blue pigment mixed with oil which becomes the sky, the sentence which becomes the motionlessly suspended cloud formation, the actor who becomes Macbeth. It is also the method of physical reality – a smooth and round cell divides and divides again and turns into the mane of a horse, a horse dies and rots and turns into soil. And it is the method of our categorising gaze – a wooden board gets four legs and becomes a stool, the stool gets a back and becomes a chair. The chair is painted and becomes a throne which in all its ordinariness there in the painting still signifies God, by the same logic that in Kiefer's work turns a hospital gown into an angel, a bathtub into an ocean, a table with coffee cups and the remains of a meal into the ship of the Argonauts.

Eventually we went over to the other house, along a three-metre-long bridge connecting them and down into the kitchen, where Lena was, and where we ate chicken soup for lunch. They told me that their neighbour had died the day before, an older woman who had lived in a dilapidated house just beyond theirs. A huge black dog pushed its head against my knees and tried to lay it in my lap. They let it out and it ran down the road, but soon it was at the door on the other side and came into the house again. I told them about our dog, which we finally had to give away, what a relief that had been. Then I told them about the Munch exhibition I was preparing and invited them to the opening. They had seen a fantastic Munch exhibition in London, they said, the self-portraits in particular had been striking. I told them this exhibition wouldn't be fantastic, that it contained only unknown works that didn't look like Munch's.

As I was leaving, I stopped in front of a picture on the wall, a print.

– It's Peter Doig, Stephen said. – Do you like him?

I nodded.

– He's interested in Munch, Stephen said. – Have you heard of the Group of Seven?

– No?

– They were a group of Canadian landscape painters who broke with naturalism in the 1920s and who were influenced by Munch, among others. Doig grew up in Canada and many of his pictures were inspired by the Group of Seven. So Munch may have had a kind of third-hand influence on him.

The first thing I did when I got home was to browse through my books of Peter Doig's pictures. I had never thought before that they had anything to do with Munch. Perhaps mainly because Doig's pictures belong to our time, I thought as I leafed through them. They relate to our reality, a world I have in common with them, that is what I saw and felt: I saw a picture of a house on a grey day, and a Sunday mood of emptiness and housing developments rose in me. There was little separating what the picture represented from my own experience of it. But what did that quality, the contemporaneity of it, consist of?

I looked at a painting entitled *Blotter*, from 1993. It depicts a boy dressed in a quilted jacket and mittens, he is standing on an ice-covered pond, the landscape around him is covered in snow, a narrow road leads past the pond and behind it stands a forest, sparse as deciduous forests are in winter. There is water on the ice, and the boy is standing with his head bent staring down at the surface.

It was very recognisable, I might have stood the same way as a boy, and I must have seen many boys standing like that, although I couldn't remember anyone specifically, for a central aspect of this picture is that it shows something from the world which we don't remember, one of the moments that don't stick in our minds but we still recognise when we see them. Typical of many of Doig's pictures from the 1990s is that they are emptied of information; they might depict empty houses or empty landscapes which at first glance don't seem to have anything noteworthy about them, as if they sought to discover just how little information is needed in order for a feeling to arise. Due to the lack of information the pictures are mysterious and often faintly menacing, many seem connected with meaninglessness and loss of the past or death. But also with boredom and triviality. If you look at them for a long time, however, things might start to happen, often in the planes surrounding the motif, for example the verticality of the tree trunks, a shape found in so many of Doig's pictures, or the materiality of the painted snow – or, as in this picture, the materiality of the painted water. The patterns, the distortions, the irregularities. The picture moves between the commonplace and the foreign without the foreignness becoming unusual, on the contrary it merges with the emptiness, or perhaps is the very thing which expresses the emptiness.

In nearly all of Munch's pictures, even in the landscapes emptied of meaning, there is a certain solemnity, perhaps only through the act of selection, as if the picture is saying, I have seen *this*. And that this is thereby elevated, by becoming art. Doig's pictures seem to be striving to eliminate the solemnity, and if so, it must be because they can give a truer picture of reality without it. In Munch the world comes out to meet us, with Doig it is neutral in terms of meaning, closer to ground zero, which of course should not be understood as something in the world itself, for the world is full of shapes and patterns, light and shadow, but rather as something within ourselves when we look at it. It is possible to think that art itself has charged it, and that Doig's pictures from the 1990s use art to neutralise the charge, that this is why the information they contain is minimised as far as is possible without the world itself disappearing. Their contemporaneity lies in the absence of solemnity, for solemnity is no longer a part of our lives; the vertical axis running between man and God, man and the sublime, man and fate, has become historical, in that we now relate to the horizontal, to the grid, where everything is connected at the same level. But what Doig retains even as he neutralises the world is the mood it gives off. The resonance of a rainy day, the resonance of a snow-filled sky, the resonance of a deserted road outside an empty house.

Other of Doig's pictures seek the iconic, but not in order to capture the universally human, as Munch did, Doig attempts rather to capture visually striking moments. A man in a red canoe on a blue ocean with a green island in the background. A man walking along a wall carrying a parasol. A girl high up in a tree with long branches. Or the wonderfully evocative picture of a red articulated lorry crossing a field with dense forest in the background as twilight falls. That painting, which is called *Hitch-Hiker* and is from 1989, wakens some of the same feelings as Munch's *Cabbage Field*.

But if one looks at Munch's and Doig's paintings side by side, the differences are often greater than the similarities. Isn't the connection merely that both painted figuratively, people and landscapes, and that the commonalities between them belong to figurative painting itself, in the most general sense?

That's what I thought until I saw Doig's painting *Echo Lake* from 1999. It is so like Munch's painting *Ashes* from 1895 that it can't be a coincidence, Doig's must be a direct reference to Munch's picture.

Ashes shows a woman lifting her hands to her head in a wild and desperate gesture, with her hair loose and looking straight ahead. Next to her a man dressed all in black is seated, his head bent. The male figure is cut off below the waist and everything about him signals a turning away: the blackness, the bowed head, the missing facial features. Around them there are light-coloured rocks, behind them the forest stands like a dark wall. No horizon, just the vertical tree trunks and the darkness shutting them in.

Echo Lake depicts a man standing on a beach in front of a lake, with black forest behind him. He is lifting his arms in the same way as the woman in *Ashes*, but he is seen at a greater distance, so the gesture might be expressing something very different, he might for example have shaped his hands into a megaphone – a possibility suggested to me by the title. Some metres behind him to the left a police car is parked, while a few metres behind him to the right there is a tree which repeats the shape of the male figure – or the shape of the woman in *Ashes* – only enlarged.

The forest, the rocks, the iconic posture is the same, and even though Doig's picture contains other things too – a lake, a police car, a lamp post – we are definitely in the same pictorial world. Doig's world is filled with something else, for while Munch's picture tells a story about a man and a woman, about desire and desperation, about openness and closedness, and about the loneliness that can arise between people, Doig's picture tells a story about a policeman who has driven to a lake, got out of his car and is standing in front of it. That story is commonplace and very particular, the generality lies in what *Echo Lake* takes from *Ashes* as a kind of stage or scene for the human, where the human isn't fixed, as in Munch – for there is no escaping that situation, it belongs to the universally human, that is what Munch's picture expresses – but is something that can appear in ever-changing forms. What kind of power do the place, the trees, the forest, the beach, the emotions that flow through us really have over what we are? Doig's picture seems to ask – but only if we set it next to Munch's picture one hundred years older.

*

Art is as much about searching as it is about creating. But if so, for what? For entrances to reality, openings into the world. When sometime during 1885 Munch began to paint a picture of a dying girl in her sickbed, the problems he posed himself were essentially the same as Peter Doig's or Stephen Gill's. Form determines what can be shown or said.

So what does one do when the determining form makes it impossible to say what one wants to say, show what one wants to show? Then the form has to be broken down, has to be destroyed. Then one is forced in a sense to become an iconoclast. For only when the form has been broken down can a new form arise, allowing room for what until then did not exist, or what until then there was no room for. Then a new entrance to reality has been created.

Far and away the best book on Munch I have read is about this. I found it by chance in the shop at the Munch Museum a few months ago, it was somewhat hidden away on the shelves, and since I had never heard of it, I took it out. It lacked the colourful and visually attractive dust covers which art books often have. Something that looked like an X-ray image of *The Sick Child* dominated the otherwise entirely black cover of the book, which was entitled *Edvard Munch: An Exposed Life* and was written by Stian Grøgaard. I had seen the name before but knew nothing about him, though I vaguely associated him with art criticism and the weekly newspaper *Morgenbladet*. I browsed through the book, decided it couldn't do any harm to buy a copy, and on the train to Gardermoen airport that afternoon I began to read. I read while I waited for my flight, I read sitting in the plane, I read on the train to Ystad, and if it hadn't been so dark in the taxi home from the train station I would have read there too.

The avidness with which I read this monograph on Munch reminded me of the greed that sometimes came over me while I was studying more than twenty years ago, not litera-ture but art history. Literature is writing, it is invariably couched in language, which literary theorists can channel and explore but rarely if ever revolutionise. After all, there are only so many ways of reading *Madame Bovary*. Visual art is languageless, theories about it are presented in a very different medium, which doesn't touch the original work. The language of theory can be more or less relevant of course, closer or more distant, but the reflections it presents are always something wholly other than the experience one has when looking at a picture. This is obvious. The books and texts which made me greedy, which made me feel that I was on to something, were often about the basis of a work of art, its genesis, the moment when it goes from being nothing to being something. Martin Heidegger's essay *The Origin of the Work of Art* was one such text, because it was so simple, not simple to understand but simple in the sense that all its concepts and its entire thinking concerned entities that were simple and familiar to everybody. *Statues* by Michel Serres was another; of all the books I have read, this is probably the one I have quoted from most often. And a short essay by Deleuze about becoming, entitled 'Literature and Life', printed in the Danish magazine *Kritik* sometime during the 1990s, which I have returned to for nearly twenty years now, where among other things he writes, 'To become is not to attain a form (identification, imitation, Mimesis) but to find the zone of proximity, indiscernibility, or undifferentiation . . .'

What these texts did, I think, was to find words for something I didn't know that I knew. That I read Grøgaard's book about Munch with the same avidity is because it focuses on the actual genesis of the paintings with a technical expertise that I lack, and it does so soberly – for a picture being painted is never great, hasn't been canonised or mythologised, it is something else and far lesser, something concrete, a canvas in a room, unfinished and changeable. 'Munch' is a static entity, so great and autocratic that it is barely in contact with anything but itself. What Grøgaard does is to bring 'Munch' into contact with the world again, and he does so in two ways: firstly by moving in a distinctly practical way closer to the situation Munch was in when he painted individual pictures – Grøgaard himself trained to be a painter, and when he writes about Munch's pictures he does so based on the technical challenges that Munch was confronted with and the technical means he had at his disposal, how they are resolved or not in the painting. What was he trying to do? What did he succeed in doing? Why, why not? This practical viewpoint sees the picture as unfinished, as something that still hasn't come into being, and thus takes away everything finished, that is, elevated and iconic, that Munch's art is burdened with. This practical viewpoint also brings the picture into contact with other pictures that were painted at the same time, and thereby with the time in which they were painted.

The other way in which Grøgaard brings the pictures into contact with the world is through theory, philosophical aesthetics, in other words by drawing them into the realm of the general and the universal, that which is true of all art.

I have never come as close to an understanding of Munch as when I read this book, precisely because it doesn't focus on the finished pictures, in other words the pictures as they appear to us, but on the problems that working on them posed, that is, the pictures as they appeared to Munch. Grøgaard's reasoning cuts like a knife through the general reception of Munch. Reading about Munch in this way is like being sober at a party where everyone else is drunk. About the portrait of his sister that he painted at the age of nineteen, for example, Grøgaard writes:

Inger in Black 1884 is a half-length portrait in a black dress painted against a black background. The face and the hands are the only parts that stand out in another colour. The torso itself proved recalcitrant. Even at the lower end of the scale the bright light upon the dress appears exterior to it, and it is too sharply cut off against the neck, an insensitivity that is repeated in the red necklace. The face alone makes up the painting, and it seems almost to loosen from the rest of the head. Pink and yellow predominate – too yellow – with a few cool shaded areas with hints of black. The slightly too warm skin may be due to transparent colour applied to parts of the painting, possibly in raw sienna, but is counterbalanced by some acidic mixed hues. Apart from this, Inger has large eyes reflecting the light, always fascinating and easy to resort to. That the face separates itself from the rest of the figure and becomes the whole painting is actually the one thing one doesn't forget about *Inger in Black*. This doesn't have to be a criticism, at least not based on the criteria which the picture itself establishes.

Despite these features, which give away the novice, the banal contrast of light works well. Portraits are said to be penetrating, and that is no cliché in the case of *Inger in Black*. The painting is made with a seriousness that no naturalist of the previous generation would have owned up to.

Yet seriousness is not what the painting was intended to convey. First and foremost it was meant to demonstrate skill as an observer in a more public format, of a model whose time was at Munch's disposal. The liberal use of black creates a mood which likely is not yet neoromantic, in the sense of ideologically conscious and opposed to the aesthetics of Krohg's generation. The colour black is an exaggeration, an economical move intended to avoid too many variables in a larger format.

The model probably had to endure hours in front of the easel, in mute solidarity with the eldest son in the family, who had already made his debut at the National Art Exhibition (Høstutstillingen). As in many of Munch's portraits, the face is of a different – both distant and insistent – order, while the rest of the figure is more perfunctory and here a little clumsy. This is due not only to a groundless materiality and problems in describing volume through nuances of light and shade, but also because Munch cannot make up his mind whether to treat black as colour or tone (atmosphere), that is, an invisibility which functions only as a margin for the penetrating portrait. The grey fields in the lighter areas of the dress, which seem to float in front of the body, reveal his difficulty in completing the figure. Black as tone provides a licence and postpones the articulation, but he fell short once black had to be modulated into volume.'[4]

Where I see a masterpiece that moves me deeply every time I look at it, and which gives me hope because the dignity she radiates is not merely hers – I mean the biographical

Inger Munch's – but something which exists always as a possibility within the human, Grøgaard sees the laborious efforts and failures of a young painter. One perspective does not exclude the other, and what makes Grøgaard's analysis so interesting is not his pointing out of the picture's unsuccessful elements in itself, but what the fact that they are there can tell us. Grøgaard's thesis is that the painterly strategies which to Krohg and Frits Thaulow's generation were self-evident and which a talent like Munch's should have easily mastered, are self-evident no more. 'What is lacking,' he writes, 'are visual *formulas* for accessing the model.'

All figurative painting is about observation and simplification, for the amount of detail in even a small segment of reality, for instance a human face, is nearly infinite, and the simplification, or the reduction of information, what to include and what not to include and in which way, occurs in accordance with certain systems, what Grøgaard calls visual formulas. What he identifies in Munch's youthful works is that the visual formulas of tradition are no longer obvious, a divergence has emerged between what Munch sees and what he paints, and a number of technical problems arise in the paintings. At the same time it is never just the motif that he is considering, but also what is happening in the painting, what he simplifies and what he paints in detail, something he must continually connect with what he wants with the painting, what he wants to attain, what makes it 'good'. This responsiveness to what is happening in the painting, this eye for possibilities that open up along the way, was perhaps one of the things that distinguished him from his contemporaries. Several of them were better trained than Munch, and Grøgaard believes that is an important factor in understanding why he in particular became so radical; painting a model's face was less straightforward for Munch and consequently occasioned more problems in his work than in that of other painters, problems which had to be solved individually and in each separate case.

Another important factor was his sensitivity, and not just that he was finely tuned to his surroundings – what we call impressionable, that he registered the surrounding mood – but also that the slightest external touch could set off a storm of emotions within him. Painting must have been a way of coping with this, perhaps primarily by making it stop, for when one paints one's own self disappears, but also by emphasising what was good about his sensitivity, which is apparent in the early paintings' desire for colour and materiality and unalloyed delight in creation – take *Garden with Red House* or *Morning*, the joy found in those pictures. But if one considers *Inger Munch in Black*, there Munch is closer to something essential, which quite eclipses the technical difficulties. That he is closer to himself and his own life doesn't make the painting more true than *Morning*, but more significant, something he himself must have realised or at least sensed. When shortly after he began painting the picture that at first was simply called *Study* but later became known as *The Sick Child*, he moved further in towards the personal without shying away from the grief that forms a kind of background to the portrait of Inger. The two levels, the personal memory of his older sister's death and the sickroom of naturalist genre painting, were impossible to reconcile, and Grøgaard uncovers this conflict practically brushstroke by brushstroke in the painting.

Munch painted *The Sick Child* using a model, but he was

looking for something other than what he had in front of him, searching for a way which could bring together what he had seen, or rather felt, with what he was seeing, the model in a room. In other words he had available to him a painterly idiom, Krohgian naturalism, which was inadequate to what he wanted to do, so he was forced to search for another one while he painted.

The result is a picture which at one and the same time comes into being and is destroyed, and the destruction, the distortion, enters into the subject matter of the painting, which is tuberculosis, a wasting disease, that is, the destruction of life, and moreover does so intransigently, with no possibility of reconciliation, since reconciliation lies in the space, here almost cancelled out through the close-up of the child and the woman and by the surface character of the painting.

Munch himself wrote about the painting,

When I saw the sick child for the first time – the pale head with the vibrant red hair against the white cushion – it made an impression that disappeared as I worked on it. I achieved a good yet different picture on the canvas. I painted the picture numerous times in the course of a year – scraped it – dissolved it in generous applications of paint – and endeavoured again and again to attain the first impression. The quivering mouth – the translucent pale complexion – against the canvas – the quivering mouth – the quivering hands. I finally ceased – exhausted. I had achieved a great deal of the first impression. The quivering mouth – the translucent skin – the weary eyes. Yet the colour of the picture was not complete – it was pale grey. The picture had become heavy as lead.

I took it up again two years later – then I achieved more of the vibrant palette that I had wished to give it. I painted three different ones. These are all different from one another and each contributes something to elicit what I felt during the first impression . . .

I had overdone the chair and the glass – it distracted from the head. When I first looked at the picture I could only make out the glass and the surroundings. Should I remove it completely? No, it contributed to deepening and accentuating the head. I scraped away the surroundings halfway and allowed them to remain as masses, which one could see above the head and glass.

I discovered furthermore that my own eyelashes had contributed to the visual impression. I therefore included a hint of them as shadows on the surface of the picture. The head became the picture in a way – wavy lines appeared in the picture – in the peripheries – with the head as the central element. I often made use of these wavy lines later.[5]

As Grøgaard points out, Munch wrote this many years later and it is marked by *ex post facto* rationalisation, he sees the painting in the light of what he painted later and includes *The Sick Child* in the Frieze of Life in a kind of self-canonisation. In any case it remains a key picture in Munch's *oeuvre*, and fairly unique in that the break with paradigm is so visible, represents such a major part of the painting's character, it is almost as if the battle between the two spaces, the inner subjective and the outer objective, can be seen. One is brought close to the process itself, what it is to paint, what a painting is, for the conflict has not been resolved, it remains open: between the will to express and the means of expression, the very basis of art, is visible. In periods when a single paradigm holds sway that basis is not visible, the connection between what is expressed and how it is expressed seems obvious, the form appears natural, as unproblematic as the shape of the hand or the foot. Here, where the divergence is so great, form becomes a problem, and we understand that it *always* is, that it is never natural, always arbitrary.

Yet the greatness of the painting is not found here, at least not as I see it. Its greatness lies in the two figures and the relation between them, in the girl's tender gaze, how she, who is dying, looks comfortingly or encouragingly at the mother, who will be left behind and is sitting with her head bent and her arm on the daughter's arm. The absence of a unified space leaves the figures somewhere between the realistic, that which relates to reality, and the iconic, and makes them movable, as if one moment they belong to the specific, the personal – it is *this* child and *this* mother at *this* very moment – and the next moment to the general, in other words that the feeling of grief, loss, courage, reconciliation to death and denial of death have been given iconic form.

The different possibilities inherent in the figures open up for different types of identification and relevance, and it is this openness, or this not-yet-closedness, which makes the painting so alive: the conflict, both in terms of motif and of form, is reawakened every time the picture is viewed. We can view other paintings of similar motifs from the same period and judge them good or less good, but from a distance, and if we involve ourselves in the emotions that have been invested in them, that is a choice we make, we don't have to. When we stand in front of *The Sick Child*, that choice doesn't exist. To look at it is to set it going.

The space in which *The Sick Child* exists, with all its ambivalences, is not a place a painter can remain in for very long, there is so much there that is unrealised, it is nearly all a searching for form and no form. It is an interstice. At the same time I think it is true to say that all artistic work at some stage is there, in the moment before something becomes something else, before it falls into place in a form and is locked to it.

If we move ahead ten years in time, to the mid-1890s, we see that Munch has found a solution to the problems he wrestled with as a twenty-year-old. These pictures are radically simplified; as Grøgaard points out, they are no longer based on meticulous observation of models or landscapes. The faces tend towards the detail-less and non-individual, many of them are merely pale fields with dark shadows for eyes, moonlight on a nocturnal surface of water is a yellow pillar, stones are beige and brown circles, indicated and referred to rather than seen and painted.

It was this aesthetic that allowed Munch to say that he didn't paint what he sees but what he saw. It was also this aesthetic that made Poul Erik Tøjner, the director of the Louisiana Museum of Modern Art, compare Edvard Munch with Andy Warhol; everything is on the surface. Munch's paintings from the 1890s are charged to the highest degree, but they are not charged with reality, it isn't visual reality they bring us close to, but emotional reality, which is transmitted through symbols. The remainder of naturalism and tradition in *The Sick Child*, that which made an identification with something other than emotion possible, is completely absent. This means that the essential thing does not take place in relation to any concrete reality, nor in the painting itself, in its painterly aspects – there is nothing to immerse oneself in there, since it is so schematic – but solely in the emotions it elicits.

*

I remember well the first time I saw Munch's pictures. It was in Oslo, at the National Gallery, I was in my late teens and up till then had hardly visited a single museum, nor was I particularly interested in art. Music and literature were my thing, but not due to any hunger for understanding or longing for insight – music was partly a means to define my identity, it said something about who I wanted to be, and partly a place where emotions were given free rein, where all the moods I had within me could be unleashed, without me ever reflecting on it, the relationship was an unconscious one, while literature was primarily an escape from reality, the joy at being able to step into other and unknown worlds.

I don't remember why I was in Oslo, nothing of the context has been preserved in my memory, but presumably it was on a trip with my *gymnas* class. What I remember are all the national romantic paintings, that I was delighted with them and impressed by how true they were to nature. And then I remember how the room with Munch's paintings knocked them out. That Munch's paintings had such a powerful aura that they overshadowed all the others. It was as if they existed on another, higher plane. This I felt to be beyond doubt, that as works of art they were better, although I had never reflected on what art was, or what quality was. I just knew it. As an experience it reminded me of when I read Dostoevsky for the first time, the feeling of acute relevance was the same.

While the preceding paintings had opened up to me and as it were received my gaze, with Munch's paintings it was the other way round, it was as if they came towards me, that they were active while my gaze was passive. That kind of intensity, that a picture could take possession of a room and dominate it, was something I hadn't experienced before. They were trembling!

That initial experience has been present in me whenever I have seen those Munch paintings again, but fainter and less intense each time. I imagined that this was due to the paintings' status, that they are so well known that what they contain vanishes behind their fame, which I bring with me when I view them, so that they are already finished within me and therefore little or nothing happens when the initial effect wears off.

Not until I read Grøgaard's book did I realise that it might be due to something in the paintings themselves, that they were finished beforehand and therefore closed. That they lived in their effect, which diminished with each viewing. And that this is why Symbolism became a dead end, a kind of backwater of art which the main current left behind and never returned to. It would not be Munch's paintings from the 1890s that led to modernism, but Paul Cézanne's.

This idea is in line with my own experience as a writer, namely that it has to happen in the actual writing, that it must always remain open to the unpredictable and the accidental, which establishes patterns that the text then follows, and that this process has to be intuitive and subject to continual improvisation. Writing cannot merely reconstruct a moment, it must itself be a moment, only then is it in touch with the world, not as depiction but as action. In other words, the distance between thought and emotion and language must be as small as possible. And the same, I suppose, is true of painting. That the art of painting is seeing and then making the distance between the seen and the painted as minimal as possible. Think of a musician who is one with his instrument, one with the music, think of Miles Davis, think of Glenn Gould, think of Aretha Franklin. No time for thought, no time for calculation, everything happens now, in the moment, in one movement, one stream. Fundamental to all creation is that it is not about transferring something one possesses and wishes to express, but about what is expressed emerging as something in itself. Only then can it come alive. It must not exist beforehand but come into being in the moment it is expressed. If that happens, it will also come into being in the moment we see it or read it, and it is this coming into being which justifies a word like 'alive' used about art and literature, which in themselves are merely dead colours on a dead canvas or dead letters on a dead book page. Knowledge is therefore not an advantage for an artist, because knowledge exists beforehand. Experience, intuitive, bodily experience, on the other hand, is crucial. It wasn't merely to learn how a body is constructed that artists previously drew countless nude studies, it was also so that they would learn to draw without thinking, to minimise the distance between the gaze and the hand.

*

This notion, that what is expressed doesn't have to do with transferring but with coming into being, I saw formulated for the first time in the above-mentioned essay by Deleuze, in a passage which I underlined: 'To write is certainly not to impose a form (of expression) on the matter of lived experience. Literature rather moves in the direction of the ill-formed or the incomplete, as Witold Gombrowicz said as well as practiced. Writing is a question of becoming, always incomplete, always in the midst of being formed, and goes beyond the matter of any liveable or lived experience. It is a process, that is, a passage of Life that traverses both the liveable and the lived.'[6]

When I read Deleuze's short essay for the first time in 1995, I didn't know how to write. I made up stories, and nothing happened in the language except what advanced the story. I thought out what was going to happen, and I rewrote sentences to make them serve the story better. Technically they were meaningful, and the language wasn't that bad, but it was as if they were created beyond myself and existed there – one image to suggest this way of writing might be a laboratory in which the objects being studied are kept in a glass case, within which they are manipulated by scientists by means of a pair of fixed gloves, the only physical connection between them and the object of their work. That is what my writing was like, like something on the other side of a glass wall, touched through a pair of stiff gloves.

That I underlined the Deleuze passage must have been because it accorded with something I knew, in that vague, undefinable and latent way one sometimes knows things. And then, one year later, something happened. I changed my language, from a radical form of *bokmål* (one of the two official forms of written Norwegian) to a more conservative form, so that what I wrote felt slightly foreign, and that space, between my real self and the 'I' of the text, made me feel freer, suddenly things happened in the text which I hadn't foreseen, which I had never thought before, and at once I knew that *this* was writing. I looked at it, it didn't express me or my world, it expressed the text, what had happened there at that particular moment. That moment could not be reconstructed, it belonged solely to the situation in which it had emerged. The art of writing was to find another such moment, and then another and another again.

The result became my first novel. It is the work of a beginner, and it is blemished by an at times obtrusive self-infatuation, the joy of being able to write. Moreover it has an air of naivety about it, but so does everything I have written since, I recognise it at once on the rare occasions when I reread something I have written. The naivety is a consequence of this way of writing, that I try to evade reflection, never think about how something seems or looks, but be as free in the moment as at all possible. Reflection is the opposite of naivety, but also of life, of which it is the superstructure.

I am not describing this experience in such detail because I think it is universally valid, but because it forms the background to how I understand Munch's pictures. When at the beginning of this book I wrote about the conflict between what exists beforehand and what comes into being without precedent, and how this was absolutely fundamental to Munch, this is where it came from. And when I call some of Munch's pictures from the 1890s 'closed', it is for the same reason.

I assume that the parameters of Munch's era were different but just as powerful. And the striking thing about Munch's *oeuvre* is that he fought free of them and found something that was his own – not without resonance with the rest of the age of course, but without obvious models – which he later left behind to paint very different pictures during the last forty years of his life, when it seems that less was at stake, where he himself took up less space, and where nothing was centred any longer.

At the same time that he sought his way into the open in this way, he continued to paint the old motifs again and again. He must have done so because he thought he could, because it seemed relevant. Thus, he cannot have seen the process, the actual coming into being, which is so visible in *The Sick Child*, as the most important thing. Presumably, what he took away from *The Sick Child* was the opposite, namely the iconic, *that* is what he found there and learned from. The girl's gaze, the mother's bent neck – *that* was the essence. He found his way to the iconic, which as soon as it was found, could be repeated, since it wasn't the way there that was essential, that is, the changeable, but the opposite, what was unchanging about it.

Poul Erik Tøjner writes about this in his book *Munch in his Own Words*:

This may be the key to the 'Munchian mystery' – to that tormented search for escape from the encroaching world. Perhaps it is possible to imagine that works of art have a share in certain ideas, so that these ideas in a certain sense have independent life, but can only be seen when they are put into practice? Munch can. And that, so to speak, becomes his final formula for a successful picture: that it exists – and then it must be made.

When Munch had sold a picture it was not unusual for him to recall it for a while, making a replica of it for himself. Neither was it unusual for him to make several versions of the same picture, and the serial nature of his printmaking production speaks for itself in this connection. His whole working method indicates this strangely metaphysical approach: pictures are found, and are made, in that order. He often took a canvas and sketched on it, then took a new one when he had the feeling that a picture had been found. At that point it was simply a question of carrying it out.[7]

That Munch so often copied his own paintings has always seemed an oddity in his artistic career, and I have thought of it as a blemish, a form of cowardice, that he clung to what he had once made back when he was innovative and in the centre of things. It had never struck me as a possibility that he might actually have considered the replicas as having the same value as the originals, that it was their iconic aspect that had value, that is, the motif itself and its form, and that finding them was the artistic achievement, as Tøjner suggests. That would also explain why after painting *The Sick Child* he didn't turn towards a more processual approach and focus on the materiality of painting, which was another obvious possibility latent in it, and which other contemporaneous painters such as Monet and Cézanne moved towards, but instead towards the symbolic and literarily illustrative.

Monet and Cézanne also worked with repetition and seriality – Monet with his haystacks and his church facade, Cézanne with his *Mont Sainte-Victoire* – but in these pictures the repetition of the motif is a way of establishing differences between them, of relativising them in relation to the varying effects of light in the course of one day and to different viewpoints and variations of the seasons, in other words of dissolving the spatial into time, which also includes the artist himself, who in every picture is present in a way that makes simple repetition impossible, since faced with the motif the painting is created anew each time.

Munch for his part did not paint the motif again but rather the painting, as if it was unaffected by him or by the time that had passed, captured once and for all. So to him the picture cannot have been relative, it must have been the opposite: essential. And if we consider what he wrote about the creation of *The Sick Child*, that is in fact what he says. First he saw an image, which disappeared as he worked on it, and the rest of the years-long process was about finding again that image, which he had within him and which was nearly unaffected by what he had in front of him. The painting is finished when it touches on the image he first saw. Then it exists and can be repeated in every other possible medium without being diminished by the multiplication.

Many of Munch's paintings from the 1890s have this distinctly iconic character, for example *Vampire* with its visual fusing of the female and the male, or *The Scream* with its striking emblem of anxiety, the open mouth and the hands pressed to the ears, or *Jealousy* with the anguished face in front of the couple in the background. *Puberty* with the naked, vulnerable girl sitting with her knees together, her arms protectively crossed and a large shadow looming to her right, *By the Deathbed* with the five heads hovering over the coffin.

None of these paintings are about facing something without preconceptions and then painting what one sees. Nor are they about the process of creating the painting or about its painterly aspects; the centred figures dominate everything else, the rest is there merely to emphasise what the figures represent. The pictures strive towards the most precise expression of a state or a phenomenon, they search for the point where everything can be brought together, and this makes them extremely monologic internally, closed to everything else in the world but the one thing they represent. And the landscapes they are set in have an air of seriality about them – the background in *The Scream* is also the background in *Despair, Anxiety* and *Sick Mood at Sunset, Despair*, while the line of the beach forms the background in, for example, *Melancholy, Woman, Summer Night's Dream (The Voice)* and *Separation*, and through repetition appears as a stage set where interchangeable events occur. All this, both that the figures are supposed to represent something universal and that the space they inhabit is serial, diminishes their uniqueness, and comes in addition to the *Jugendstil* quality of the wavy lines, which belong to the time and the culture as much as to the painter.

According to my aesthetic preferences, or what in literary terms is called poetics, all of these aspects are weaknesses of the paintings. What Deleuze wrote – 'To write is certainly not to impose a form (of expression) on the matter of lived experience' – is exactly what Munch does in his paintings from the 1890s. Furthermore, in the world of literature a dominant idea, which I have always shared, is that only what cannot be transposed into other media is of literary value. Quality lies in what is specific to the medium – you can't successfully film a novel by Jon Fosse because the essential thing in his novels lies in the writing, that is where the essential is expressed. In Munch's paintings from the 1890s it is the other way round – he searches for precisely those forms of expression which can be transposed into other media, and reduces his pictures to the lowest common denominator of expression, which is the iconic, as both Grø-gaard and Tøjner point out. And Munch also transposes in the other direction – he transposes elements typical of litera-ture into pictures, and he creates spaces resembling those found in the theatre.

But these are arguments. And you can't argue against feelings. For despite their weaknesses, despite the obvious banality, Munch's paintings from the 1890s possess unique emotional power. And their monologic quality makes it impossible to remain unaffected by this emotional power; for that one would have to turn one's back on the paintings. It is precisely everything that is wrong with them, aestheti-cally speaking, which makes them effective: that they are closed in on themselves, have no real pictorial space and are almost exaggeratedly iconographic.

Every time I look at *Melancholy* I am struck by the mild and mournful waves in the sky, they also arise within me, in a place far beyond the reach of reflection. Then, when reflec-tion intervenes, it might be with the thought that the sad face in the foreground actually looks rather foolish and makes the painting a bit silly, as if thought wants to correct feeling, to shame it. Every time I look at the woman and the man on the beach, I am struck by their loneliness, and my own loneliness attaches itself to theirs, but not in a painful way, it is more that I catch sight of it and realise that it is a fundamental condition shared by everyone, something life is really about overcoming. For all these paintings are existentially charged, and their charge lies in their emotional power, which overshadows the otherwise banal. That, I think, is the only reason Munch's pictures in particular have survived from that time and stylistic epoch. Symbolism itself was dead almost before it emerged.

The comparison with Dostoevsky's novels still seems relevant to me, for Dostoevsky placed as little weight on the description of rooms and landscapes, the construction of scenes and the development of his characters as Munch did on pictorial space and the people within it, and for the same reason: they both wanted to get straight to the urgent and important thing, what was burning within them. Compared to his contemporary Tolstoy's novels, Dostoevsky's seem sketch-like, ramshackle, his solutions are hasty and the mood feverish, verging on the hysterical. Tolstoy describes every room and every character elaborately and fully, and regardless of how dramatic the events are, they are always rendered in meticulous detail and take place against a background which lends them depth and complexity and not least aesthetic perfection. Dostoevsky was always imperfect because he put feelings and the life of emotions before everything else. Tolstoy was the greater writer, that becomes clearer to me every time I read him, but Dostoevsky in some areas accomplished more, went deeper, into what only intensity could open up: grace, self-annihilation, the mystery of the divine. The events in his novels may be unconvincing in their melodrama, but this is overshadowed by their power.

Munch possessed the same kind of intensity, he wanted to get straight to the essential, and although his temperament was cooler, he had less insight into life, and divinity and grace were entirely absent from his pictures, still their power is so great that it nullifies aesthetic judgement. Munch's domain was not ecstasy and religion, good and evil, but life and death, woman and sexuality, and above all loneliness. I am certain that he personally sought the essential, that is the unchanging truth, but his view of woman, for example, founded as it was on fear and desire, and his view of death as an omnipresent entity, never far away from sexuality, is now apparent to us as something typical of the age, that *fin de siè-cle* atmosphere which pervaded art and literature in the final decade of the nineteenth century. It belonged to Munch and his private experience of loss, and it belonged to the age he lived in, but it doesn't belong to us. And in this too there lies a power of fascination, for that something personal and typical of the age is presented as something universal and valid for everyone, makes it seem almost monumentally alien, as if sent to us from another world: the world of loneliness, the world of sexual anxiety, the world of the death-woman temptress.

*

With his sharp and sober gaze, which sometimes places inordinate demands upon the painting, Grøgaard strips Munch bare in canvas after canvas, but he does so with respect and insight, and always with differentiation, so that *The Scream*, for example, is held above the other Frieze of

Life paintings and viewed as almost incomprehensibly ground-breaking and advanced in its wildness. Grøgaard writes that Munch struggled to maintain his standard and seems surprised whenever he actually succeeded, and I think that view of Munch must be close to Munch's own, for of course he was aware of his own limitations and knew well when he had gone beyond them. But these considerations of painterly processes, of which possibilities stood open to him, which were made use of and which were left untried, what he succeeded in and where he failed, viewed against the painting's own premises, are merely a part of the picture – the other part concerns us, the lay viewers of his paintings, and what they give us. In Poul Erik Tøjner's book on Munch that is the perspective to a greater degree, so although Tøjner identifies the same problem areas in Munch's pictures from the 1890s as Grøgaard does, he understands them differently. At times he seems almost shocked at how good they are.

Munch has the dexterity of the poster artist, yet for all that his pictures are not poster-like; he is still a painter with a grasp of the multiplicity of the senses, but first and foremost he is aware of the surface of his painting and its profound power of statement. He stamps out his subjects, and even though they may be executed with the most slovenly of brushes, they are still astonishingly accurately balanced in relation to what they are meant to express. It is like when, in the course of a long conversation, the decisive single words fall just so. Over and over again. A kind of taciturn eloquence, precision in naked form.

And then there are all the characteristics of confrontational aesthetics. Wildly unfolding, always, in Munch's work. He arranges the space with a characteristic sloping foreground. The pictures dip, and it is almost a miracle that Munch's figures haven't fallen out of the paintings over time, quite simply slid down the wall, for that's how the whole thing is constructed: the paintings are like chutes sending the depicted subject straight into the arms of the viewer. And there YOU stand, and have to answer for yourself.[8]

There are no rules in art, only conventions, and this makes judgements about quality so complicated, for criteria of quality also change of course and are based on conventions that are as difficult to see and identify as the tone of the times or the dominant pictorial language; as with these, arbitrary opinion comes to seem something natural and indisputable, at least in its broad outlines. My notions that a painting should explore that which is specific to painting, that is, colours and shapes, that literature should explore what is specific to literature, that is, writing, belong to modernism and were not operative as art theory during the 1890s, although many artistic practices embodied them. Munch's paintings from the 1890s have really always been wrong – back then they were too unfinished and too flat, now they are too banal and too medium-unspecific – and when they have seemed right, this has been based on other premises, as precursors to expressionism, for example. Paradoxically, they have also always been considered significant, works of art produced by an artist we still have to engage with.

For me the pictures have always been there in a way

which makes them easy to forget or to underestimate, which seems incomprehensible as soon as one stands in front of them again. This is so, I think, because the familiarity I feel in relation to the pictures after having seen them so many times and in so many settings is contrary to their fundamental character, which is the opposite of familiarity, namely strangeness. Realistic paintings create a sense of familiarity because they are set in a space we know, and when Munch broke with that convention it was in order to establish another, for him deeper, familiarity, through the iconic, where the figures expressed something universally true and came alive in the tension between the alien, the Sigbjørn Obstfelder-like strangeness of everything and the familiarity of the iconic.

The iconographer of strangeness, that might be an epithet for the Munch of the 1890s.

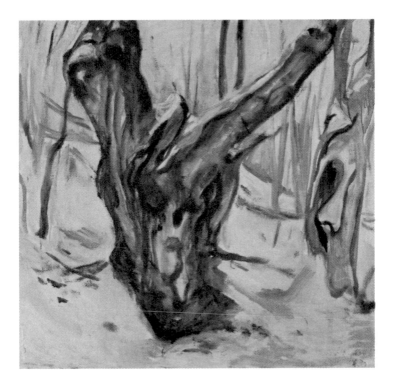

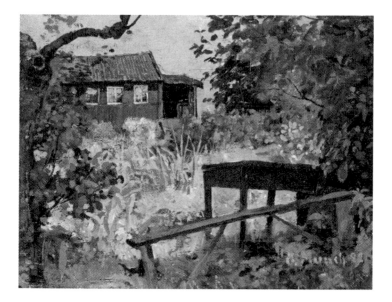

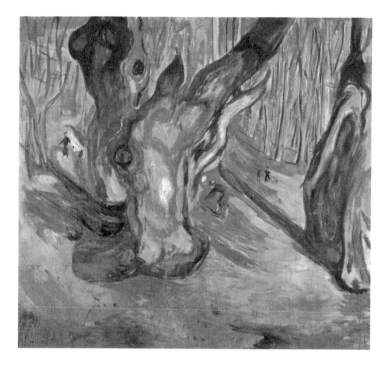

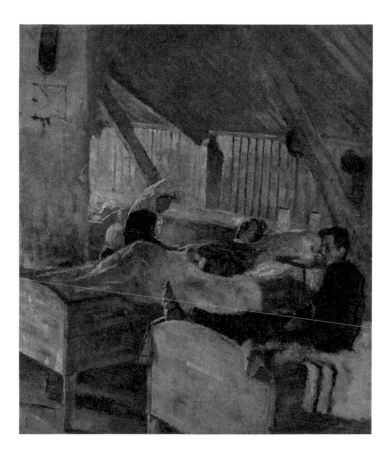

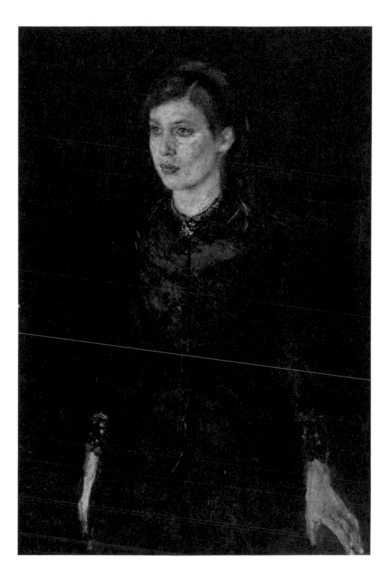

TWO

On 11 December 2013 I was sitting as I am sitting now, behind my desk, looking out at the snow-covered lawn, the sky above the trees up by the churchyard, while the light slowly began to fade. I remember the exact date because the next day I was supposed to give a speech at the House of Culture in Elverum to mark the 150th anniversary of Edvard Munch's birth in the neighbouring municipality of Løten. Also, I was keeping a diary at the time.

Only a few hours remained until I had to set off, and I still hadn't written anything I could use in my lecture. The previous weeks had been chaotic, I had been alone with the children, had had to drive here and there, the car had been at the mechanic's, one of the children was having a hard time at school, which had repercussions at home, and the kind but stupid and for me unmanageable dog had a sore on its chest that I hadn't had time to attend to. Then first one and then the other of the children's grandmothers had come here to visit, since I was going to Norway, and new tensions filled the house. I was so worn out that I only kept going out of sheer willpower, but when the day – the high point of which was always the journey home from school with the children in the car, across the fields where darkness lay like an ocean and the lights of the tractors that often drove along in the far distance filled me with peace – was over, I always sat up late in the office, I needed time to myself, it felt more important than sleep. I would sit in the chair beneath the lamp, drinking coffee and smoking and looking at the pictures in the four books I had containing Munch's collected paintings. I gazed at picture after picture, and eventually I became familiar with almost all of them, yet for all that I still couldn't come up with anything to say about them.

There are pictures of more than 1,700 oil paintings in those books, they span more than sixty-five years, a whole lifetime and two world wars. They begin in a world where the horse and cart were the usual means of transportation and end in a world with aeroplanes, cars, radios, films, cameras, submarines, aircraft carriers and rockets. They begin in a world where paintings reproduce scenes representing reality, rooms where people sit knitting or reading in the light of oil lamps, and end in a world where painting has broken away from its task of representation and become abstract. Dadaism, Futurism, surrealism and cubism have all by then briefly been the future, but are already the past.

Viewed in the light of historical and cultural developments, Munch's pictures are relatively consistent, it is possible to see or at least to understand that they were painted by the same man, but seen as a whole, as a closed pictorial universe, as Gerd Woll invites the reader to do in those four volumes, the pictures are remarkably different, and that is why I struggled to write that speech – what could I say about Munch's art that would be applicable to all his pictures? What, if anything, was the unifying element?

I thought of a Munch painting I had seen once in

Bergen, of a snow-covered landscape, I had been unprepared for it, and my eyes grew moist. I was nineteen years old, and the loneliness in the painting seemed infinite.

Now I looked it up and studied it again. It was from Thüringen in Germany, one of five motifs he painted there in 1906.

It didn't have the same effect on me now, it is something quite different to see a photographed painting reproduced in a book than to see it in reality, especially when it comes to Munch's paintings. When they are photographed their colours become dense and the paintings seem glossy, whereas in reality the colours are so thin that they barely cover the canvas and are often rather dry. This unfinished look adds to the character of each painting, it is not just a picture, it is this picture, a particular object in the world. And the unfinishedness points back to the moment the painting was made and to the person who made it.

But I wasn't thinking of that the first time I stood in front of the painting. It opened up vast spaces within me, as only art can do, when it feels as if my emotions are greater than me, that they stand open to the world, almost as if they *are* the world.

The fundamental feeling was one of loneliness, of being alone in the world. Not without friends and family, not without other people nearby, not actual tangible loneliness, but a wild and existential one: I am here, on earth, and I am here alone.

Where in this painting was loneliness? Where was it located?

The landscape was deserted, but many painted landscapes are, and yet they don't evoke a feeling of loneliness.

I assumed the reason Munch had found this landscape worthy of five paintings had to do with the snow, that the snow cover was so thin that the colours beneath shone through it everywhere. A field leads away into the picture, the whiteness is broken up by reddish and brownish stripes. To the left is a field of green, to the right a field of yellow. Beyond the field there is a downward-sloping hill, also reddish, and behind it lies a forest, painted as one continual field of dark green. The sky above is dirty white, almost yellow. The forest and a solitary tree growing at the foot of the hill distinguish this painting from the other four, which only depict fields.

Which is to say practically nothing, for what matters is that the painting is alive. It has a resonance, it oscillates, it is almost like music. This resonance is what the emotions latch on to and what lifts them, as music can lift one's emotions.

The painting blends with the feelings, a harmony arises. But only if one is open to it, if not the painting is merely a few lines and colours. It was the same thing when Munch stood before this landscape 111 years ago. He was open to it and it began to live within him, the oscillations in the landscape became oscillations in his feelings. If he hadn't been open to it, it would have been merely some lines and colours, a field and a hill.

This openness to the world is what I ended up writing about in my speech. For the world is not something in itself, ready to be observed. The world comes into being in our gaze all the time. It isn't, it becomes. It is impossible to live in this becoming, it is impossible to grasp, therefore we have developed a whole range of different ways of managing it. We call it knowledge. We know that the sky is blue and consists of air, we know that trees are green and consist of trunk, branches and leaves. We know that sand is light when it is dry and dark when it is wet. We know that sugar is grainy and tastes sweet, we know that a bathtub is smooth and hard and that water doesn't disappear into it the way it does with more porous surfaces. We know that what is far away looks small, while what is close looks big. We know that our neighbour likes to talk a lot, that one of our colleagues often uses too much eau de cologne, and roughly how heavy a shopping bag with four litres of milk in it will feel. We know what our father was like, and our mother, and we know what our friends are like. We know what it is like to climb out of a plane in southern Europe when it arrives from Scandinavia: the air is like a wall of heat. We know what a tulip looks like, and a glass of water when it has been left on the dining table after dinner and is full of little bubbles, we even know how the water will taste, lukewarm and flat. All the knowledge we have about the world acts like a shield, something we hold up against the world so as not to be overwhelmed by new impressions. It is a practical strategy, and it isn't something we think about, it applies to everyone, presumably also to animals. We can't just feel, we have to live too. Once in a while we meet someone who pierces all this, the people who change a room as they enter it, or take possession of it. They have what we call charisma, a peculiar quality that is difficult to define, it has nothing to do with looks, but rather with who they *are*. It has nothing to do with what they can do, whether they are skilled or knowledgeable, it is something more primitive than that, it is their way of being which is attractive.

However, it is also true that all people have a very

particular aura, something unique to them. Often it is barely perceptible, and in social life it can be difficult to distinguish, their aura doesn't penetrate our guard. Think of all the hundreds of faces and bodies we see when we walk through a city, how they just pass us by without leaving a trace in us. It is the same way with everything, every object or plant, every tree or landscape, every animal and every bird has its own aura, everything is unique, both in time and in space. And in the same way as with people who have a powerful charisma, we notice it when it becomes striking: the view of the mountains and fjords on the west coast of Norway makes us stop in our tracks, it can take our breath away, while the view of the outskirts of a city, with railway tracks, tufts of grass, car parks and supermarkets is something we hardly register. But this protective mechanism is not the same for everyone, in some people it is very strong, they are the robust ones, others hardly have it at all, and to them even a simple thing like travelling, with the flood of new impressions, chaos and unpredictability that entails, can be more than they can handle. And being with many people at the same time is unbearable, the different personalities and the many opposed wills are like a bombardment of the soul. Such people used to be called nervous – their nerves were too sensitive, they were thin-skinned – while nowadays we say that they are highly sensitive or, if they are paralysed by it, that they suffer from anxiety.

There is no doubt that Munch belonged to the latter category. His biographer Rolf Stenersen, who interacted with him over a period of twenty years, writes that Munch found it difficult to be with many people at the same time, he preferred to meet people singly and if possible only people he had known for a long time, and during such encounters he talked incessantly, which Stenersen thought of as another way he had of protecting himself, of shutting the other person out. This of course is the myth of the artist as being extra-delicate and sensitive, nearly unfit for life, but it has become a myth because it is so often the case. It is also relevant to our understanding of what art is, not least in regard to Munch's art and especially the five paintings from Thüringen, for that is the essential thing about them, that Munch sees what is unique about this landscape – not that it differs from other landscapes, but the unique aura it possesses, which only this place has – and this is what he paints. He stands there unprotected against it, and it arises within him. He paints his encounter with the landscape, and the note it gives rise to within him, he awakens in us.

*

After a couple of hours I had finished writing the lecture. I wasn't very pleased with it, because it was really more about all artists and all art than specifically about Munch, and because many of his pictures pointed towards something very different – no one could say that *Woman in Three Stages* stood open to the world and the unique radiance of people; on the contrary, everything in it was shut up within Munch's own mind, which was hardly in touch with reality at all in that particular painting – but I was already late, so it would have to do.

I put my suit in a garment bag, packed a small suitcase and went out into the yard. The children's grandmothers had borrowed the car and taken the dog to the vet, but they knew when I had to leave and would probably be here soon,

I thought. The plan was to pick up a friend, visit the library in Malmö and listen to an interview with a writer, have dinner with the writer and her editor afterwards, and then take the train to Kastrup airport outside Copenhagen, spend the night there, fly to Oslo the next morning, stop at my publisher's offices, take the train out to Løten and deliver my speech. I didn't want to go, didn't feel up to it, but I had to.

I was still standing in the darkness outside the house when they arrived. I picked up my friend, drove to Malmö, went into the library, it was packed, there were four hundred people in there, and we found a place to sit behind some shelves, where we could hear what was being said but not see anything.

I got a little drunk during the dinner at La Belle Epoque, I think the place was called, and didn't feel the biting cold as around midnight I walked towards the railway station. My bank card wasn't accepted by the ticket vending machine, so I got on the train without a ticket, they rarely check, but sure enough, on this particular night a conductor came, and she was angry and irritated when I explained the situation, she said she'd come back and give me a fine, but when I got off at Kastrup she still hadn't come. Slept there, got on the plane, landed at Gardermoen, took the airport train to the National Theatre, went to Oktober publishing house to meet my editor. I had brought with me a picture I had painted for his fiftieth birthday, it was embarrassing, I handed it to him wrapped in a plastic bag, he asked me whether he should look at it now or later, I said later and got an SMS when I was on the train to Løten, saying that the painting was nice and that he liked it. Oh no, how awkward. I had wanted to give him something that wasn't just an easy purchase but had required some effort, so the point wasn't really for the picture to be good. But it was a foolish thought, for who wants an amateur painting? What can you do with it except put it in the attic? It is, as is so often the case with me, thrusting yourself on other people.

Can't remember anything else from the publisher's offices that day. I remember the train, the two people who were sitting in the seats near me, at the end of the first-class compartment, and the conductor who came, and I remember this because a man from the phone company here in Skåne called while I was sitting there, he was installing fibre-optic cable and wondered where I wanted it, a conversation which was cut off after a few minutes when my mobile phone ran out of money.

At the train station in Løten a woman was waiting for me. She worked at the National Museum of Art, Architecture and Design and had studied art history, was perhaps a few years younger than me, and had a devil-may-care air about her. Said she had Tourette's syndrome, or was that just a thought that came to my mind? She asked if I wanted to come with her to the farm where Munch had been born and have coffee with the people who owned it now. I wanted to say no, I didn't want to meet anyone or talk to anyone, but I couldn't, I never can when someone asks something of me face to face.

As we drove into the farmyard, dusk was falling. The farm buildings lay on a low hill, white fields stretched out all around. The farm must have been wealthy going back a long time, and it was well kept. Plenty of buildings, storehouse and outhouses and stable and barn, and a large main house painted white. The owners were around sixty, well dressed, well suited and hospitable, and they showed us the floor upstairs where the Munch family had lived in 1863 when the father Christian worked as an army doctor in Hedmark.

What was now one large room had then been three, I gathered. But several of their pieces of furniture had been preserved, including the bed where Edvard had been born, which stood against the wall. A cabinet with doctor's implements stood by another wall.

It was completely still in there. The faint light reflected by the snow-covered fields outside barely shone through the windows.

He was born on this day, I thought. In this light and in this silence.

Much had changed during the 150 years that had passed since then, but not that.

That thought, that the light was unchanging, made it feel as if something stood open. And though I knew it was in me, it felt as if it was in the room.

Of course Munch was just another human being, and people are born all over the place all the time, but in the past few weeks I had looked at and studied his pictures so many times, in addition to reading and thinking about him a good deal, that I was close to his mental world, or perhaps rather to the states of mind through which he experienced the world, so on that afternoon I was particularly susceptible.

The woman who gave birth to him was named Laura Cathrine, she was considerably younger than Christian, and she would die only five years later, of consumption, and one of her children, Sophie, would die of consumption seven years after that, another daughter, Laura, would become mentally ill and end up in an institution, while her second son, Andreas, would die as a young man, he too of consumption. Of their flock of children only Edvard and Inger would grow old, but neither of them would live a happy life, least of all Edvard, who despite all his successes and fame remained troubled, if we are to believe Stenersen, who draws a portrait of an unhappy, inhibited man, full of longings he was unable to fulfil, as if shut out from life with others.

The Munch family belonged to the official class, Christian's paternal grandfather had been a parish priest, his father was a diocesan priest in Kristiania, his uncle was a bishop in Kristiansand, his brother was P. A. Munch, Norway's most famous historian, their cousin was the poet Andreas Munch. So even though his father had financial difficulties while Edvard was growing up, and they at times lived close to the poverty line, I imagine that Edvard's identity was linked to the standing of his family name, which would explain at least partly how as a young man of relatively limited means he could have such confidence in himself and his own talent that he was able to follow it to places none of his contemporaries wanted or were able to go.

They lived here once, in this room, Sophie, Edvard, Laura Cathrine and Christian. Little did they know that people of the future would be preoccupied with them, write books and read about their character traits, their lives and how they lived. I know more about them than I know about my own family, for the murk of history begins to gather over the parents of my grandparents, who must have been born at about the same time as Edvard Munch. There are no houses left in which they lived, no rooms where they stayed, no beds where they were born, everything has vanished into the darkness of the past.

I went over to the window and looked out at the white fields glimmering faintly in the twilight, almost completely drained of light now, turned back towards the room again, threw one last glance at the bed and went out, we were invited for coffee downstairs in the living room.

There was something so comforting about being there, I think now. December in the dusk on an old Norwegian farm, that was nice in itself, and the pictures and letters which Munch had sent to the family during the course of his life and which now hung on the walls on the ground floor, they were fine too, but what I felt was something else, something deeper, more moving, hopeful.

Perhaps that something began there, without anyone knowing it. And that something is beginning around us all the time, without us knowing.

*

Late last night, while I was selecting pictures for this book, I got an email from the artist Anna Bjerger. I have promised to write a piece for a book of her pictures which she is publishing. She had attached a file containing thirty photographed paintings, so that I had something to refer to. I had seen many of them before, but some were new to me, among them a fantastic picture of a landscape of fields, it is viewed from straight above, as if from a plane, the colours are predominantly yellow, but also orange, brown and green, the whole picture glows with colour, and the pattern of fields leading away into the background creates a delightful pull and a depth in the otherwise utterly flat landscape. Another picture, just as fantastic, as glowing with colour and as dominated by large fields, depicts a greenish ocean and a grey concrete pier where a boy in swimming trunks is sitting, his back is turned to the viewer, this motif too is viewed from above, at a slight angle. But my absolute favourite is the painting of a woman swimming underwater, the greenish and dizzying underwater space in it, the world of light one senses above her but cannot see, the green colours darkening towards the depths.

The world of Bjerger's motifs is not unlike Munch's – there are shorelines, there are fields, there are people in gardens, there are people in towns, there are portraits of faces and half-length portraits – but what they express is something very different. Whereas Munch charged all his pictures with himself – his own memories, his own moods and his own personal experiences – and did so in his own style with his own circle of motifs, so that we, if we are open to his pictures, can see what he saw and feel what he felt, Anna Bjerger uses photographs as the starting point for her paintings – not her own, but photos she finds at flea markets, in old magazines and weeklies, newspapers, books and user manuals. Her strategy is thus as far removed from Munch's as it is possible to get, it might even make sense to say that it is the exact opposite. In Bjerger's pictures the angle, the perspective, the motif and the framing have been chosen by someone else. Naturally, she invests something of herself in the choice of colours, style and the way the motif is reduced, but the personal, the deep-felt is already displaced through the difference between the person seeing and the person painting. The relation between the personal and the epochal becomes the theme of her paintings, that is what they explore and where they derive their force.

When I saw one of Bjerger's paintings for the first time I

knew nothing about this, but it was still present, there was a distance in the picture, something foreign which I was unable to locate but which still filled with me with a certain melancholy. It was probably precisely because the motifs so clearly belong to our shared visual experience, and that the impersonal in it, that stream of expectations flowing through it, which is an unacknowledged part of all of us, suddenly became visible, jolted out of the otherwise invisible context by the colours and Bjerger's style.

Why melancholy?

I saw our loneliness, not the individual loneliness that Munch painted but the collective, that which arises when we disappear into each other. We cannot disappear in that way to ourselves, but others can disappear to us, and this allows us to see that we too disappear to them.

At the same time all of Bjerger's pictures are beautiful, the colours are uniquely intense, glowing, not in the darkness but in the light. It is as if they celebrate at one and the same time the world and the loneliness within it.

I sent her some questions about who Munch was to her and whether she related to his pictures in any way in her own work, what strengths and weaknesses she saw in them, why it was that she always painted using photographs as her starting point.

I just received her reply.

I can't remember the first time I saw a painting by Munch, it is as if his paintings have always been there, in my mind. His strength lies in his absolute integrity as a painter. His language is so self-evident, so wilful and clear. In his choice of colours and shapes he was ruled by his own logic, it is impossible to categorise him. The autobiographical is always present, but it doesn't take over or become self-pitying, since his paintings are so clearly grounded in a tradition that is his own. Life and suffering are present in his brush-strokes, in the choice of colours and the composition.

I think that one goes through different stages in one's relationship to the work of other artists. It is something changeable that allows one to continually discover new things and new works that feel more relevant. Munch often went back to the same motif, that is why I tend to think of his motifs rather than of specific paintings. What I notice most in his paintings is often something purely technical, how he paints hair, a kiss, a sunset or logs in the forest (bright yellow).

In my paintings I take as my starting point a prosaic gaze that isn't my own, I use anonymous photographs as models. The universal gaze represented in these pictures interests me, since it conforms to a tradition inherited from the history of art. There is a stability and a neutrality in the motif which challenges me to make it my own, through painting it.

I am trying to remember how it came about that I began to paint from photographs, but it was something that happened gradually. In the beginning I used my own photographs, later the personal photos of others, but I decided that there was too much nostalgia in this, that wasn't what I wanted to explore.

I am interested in the transformative moment when a photographic motif is reinterpreted as a painting, how obvious one's own mood can be in brushstrokes and colour. How much information and experience a certain colour tone can convey as compared to another, and how close to the non-figurative one can get before the motif dissolves completely.

I think that my pictures are often unassertive and open to several interpretations, while Munch's pictures have a distinct and forceful aura. We don't have much in common except that we are both painters, but I would never deny that I have been influenced by his paintings. To me he is a source of inspiration because he is such an obvious example of how painting can feel intimate, relevant and intense regardless of time and space.

I just thought of a late painting, *Self-Portrait between the Clock and the Bed*, from 1940–3. He is standing erect in the door opening, an old and frail man, diagonally behind him a clock is symbolically placed. Yellow light falls into the room and spills upon the floor. It is a playful painting, it feels as if he has executed it with rapid brushwork. For some reason or other my gaze is held by the bedspread. Something moves me about the way the pattern has been painted on a nearly untouched surface. There is such gravity in this painting, and the execution of it is so contradictory. Perhaps this is what his greatness consists of, that he succeeds in changing our notions about how the great questions in life can manifest themselves.

About two years after I gave the lecture about Munch on the evening he would have turned 150 years old, in the festively decorated House of Culture in Elverum, I was contacted by the Munch Museum in Oslo, they wondered whether I would curate an exhibition for them.

Although I have never done anything similar, not even anything remotely like it, and although I didn't know exactly what it would entail, I said yes without a second thought. It was a clear case of hubris, for my only qualification was that I liked looking at paintings and often browsed through art books. The hubris was of course connected with my lack of knowledge, it is always easy to say yes to something one doesn't understand the scope of. Stupidity can also be liberating.

Some weeks later I visited the museum to have an initial meeting with them. It was late summer and sunny, I sat out on the terrace in front of the museum building together with the director of exhibitions and collections, Jon-Ove Steihaug, who took me through the very basics. That they had roughly one thousand paintings and twenty thousand prints in storage, and the major part of the exhibition would have to be based on these, but that it was also possible to borrow a few pictures from elsewhere. That there were four exhibition rooms. That the exhibition would first be done virtually, in something he called SketchUp, and that everything had to be ready a year before the opening. I realised that the museum's processes were slower than I was used to. I told him it wouldn't be a problem. Later he showed me around the four exhibition rooms and some of the other rooms that lie off long and labyrinthine corridors on several floors. The building is from the 1960s, and I liked the cumbersome and uncompromising aura it has, there were no open-plan offices or practical arrangements of rooms, and nothing to indicate that their business was visual art, just white walls and small cube-shaped rooms, brick walls, wood panelling and linoleum floors, not unlike some of the schools I went to as a child, built in the same period, based on the same notions of what an institution, a society and a human being was or should be.

In a few years the whole museum was to move to a brand-new, modern building, and that was why I had been invited to curate, Jon-Ove said, they wanted to take the opportunity to upend everything by inviting people from the outside, mostly artists such as Bjarne Melgaard, Per Inge Bjørlo and Lena Cronqvist, but also a cultural theorist, Mieke Bal, in addition to which they had had and would have a series of exhibitions which viewed Munch alongside the work of other artists such as Robert Mapplethorpe, van Gogh, Jasper Johns, Gustav Vigeland and Asger Jorn.

We arranged a further meeting, where I would present my initial thoughts for the exhibition. I already knew one thing, namely that I didn't want to show any of the famous paintings. For what had struck me as I leafed through Munch's collected works that first time was how much of it I had never seen before, how many-sided his pictures had been, and how interesting it was to follow the various currents, how they seemed to narrow and coalesce in certain motifs before they let go and flowed on into some-thing different. When I looked at the famous pictures, I saw 'Munch', when I looked at the unknown works, I saw paintings.

All Munch's paintings, including the best-known ones of course, were seen for the first time when he was still active, and in order to show who he was as a painter, I decided to try to select pictures that didn't evoke 'Munch', based on the notion that 'Munch' was an obstacle that led all thoughts and feelings into a particular form.

Was it possible to see Munch without seeing 'Munch', in other words was it possible to see him the way he was when seen for the first time? Was it still possible to view pictures by Munch without knowing what to think?

Another thing I had noticed was that he had painted so many pictures that seemed harmonious, that weren't charged with anxiety and darkness, but on the contrary were filled with sunlight and calm and people engaged in daily tasks out in the open. Bathing women and men, farmers harvesting or ploughing, sun-filled gardens, beaches and coves, horses, dogs and trees, everywhere trees, all kinds of trees, apple trees, chestnuts, elms, oaks, pines, spruces.

What if the exhibition were to begin there, with a room full of harmony? And if the landscape was then gradually emptied of people, shifting towards his empty but existentially charged landscape, and from there went on into his innermost self? And then back out again?

No chronology, no dates, no titles, no text, just a flood of pictures from the outer towards the inner and back to the outer again.

It wasn't much of a plan, but it was all I had when I met Jon-Ove again, together with the woman who would be my co-curator on the project, Kari Brandtzæg. I was so embarrassed about my proposal that I spent more time excusing it than presenting it.

They said they thought it was a good starting point. Of course they had to say that, but although I knew this, I chose to disregard that possibility, and when I got home I began to select possible pictures in four different categories: harmony, forest, the inner world, portraits.

*

At home I spent a long time cutting out pictures from the volumes of Munch's collected works, placing them on the floor in the guest house, arranging them in four imaginary rooms, moving the cuttings back and forth between the various walls and different rooms, searching for a rhythm, a connection, an interrelatedness which would move through the pictures.

Munch was concerned with seriality, all his life he put pictures in and out of the series he called the Frieze of Life; what he was interested in was how the pictures worked in relation to each other. He himself wrote as follows about this:

> I have always worked best with my paintings around me. I arranged them together and felt that some of the pictures were connected to each other in content. When they were positioned together there immediately arose a resonance between them and they became totally different than when displayed individually. It became a symphony.
>
> That is when I decided to paint friezes.[9]

If one looks at photographs of Munch from Ekely, most often he is surrounded by pictures from all periods, and the impression this gives is of a work in progress, a continual painterly movement that he is in the middle of. It is as if he lives in his painting, a little like Proust during the final years of his life lived in the novel. And if one looks at the exhibitions he held, pictures from his entire career are included, as if he didn't weigh or grade the different periods and styles against each other, but they were all part of the same. And yet it is as a painter of individual works that he is remembered. The German art historian Ulrich Bischoff writes in his book *Edvard Munch 1863–1944: Images of Life and Death*:

So central is the Frieze in Munch's work that one might conclude that his art must be understood in terms of context and sequence. But every important work of art transcends the historical moment, the social background, and the formal conditions of its creation; and this is eminently true of Munch's art too. It is the power of individual paintings that gives Munch's work its enduring force.[10]

But I can't help being fascinated by the other image, of the man who painted throughout his entire life and who in his final thirty years did so alone in large houses filled with paintings, which not only surrounded him but also depicted what surrounded him – the rooms of the house, the garden outside, the forest nearby, the image of himself in the mirror. And if one unlocks Munch's position as the painter of individual works and allows the pictures to flow, perhaps other patterns and connections will be revealed. All those people standing in the landscape with their hands stretched up towards a tree or a berry bush who thereby resemble trees themselves. All the people without facial features, those who cannot be seen. All the trees mysteriously giving shape to themselves, some of them almost dissolved into the landscape by the movements of the wind, others bare and splayed, others again full of apples. The people around the apple trees, perhaps the most frequently recurring motif in all of Munch's works, most often a man and a woman, sometimes charged with powerful emotion, sometimes not. The empty landscapes, the bare smooth rocks along the shore, the forests, the strips of land, the fields. The cabbage field, painted at dusk, the colours green-blue and dark yellow, the line heading straight into the darkness, the atmosphere of peace and death it radiates.

Taken separately, few of these paintings can compare with his most powerful paintings from the 1890s, some of them are downright weak, but together they bring with them something else, I thought. Together they tell a different story.

I also had an idea that the external forest should gradually turn into an inner forest, something chaotic and irrepressible, something untamed and almost unarticulated, and that this inner forest would be connected to the outer one through the materials, matter, art as objects. A wooden board with an image cut into it, filled with ink and pressed onto paper, a face etched into copper and printed, or into stone and printed. The oil paints' own life, the spots and the stiff lumps of impasto, the layers of paint so thin the canvas shone through.

But what kind of an entity is 'the inner' when applied to painting?

Munch himself wrote about his paintings from the 1890s:

> I painted picture upon picture in keeping with the impression made on my eye in a moment of heightened emotion – painted the lines and colours that remained fastened to my inner eye – to the retina.

I painted only what I remembered without adding anything to it – without the details that I no longer saw. Hence the simplicity of the pictures – the apparent emptiness.

I painted impressions from childhood – the faded colours from that time.

By painting the colours and lines and shapes I had seen in an emotional state – I wished to recapture the quivering quality of the emotional atmosphere like a phonograph.

This is how the pictures of the Frieze of Life came into being.[11]

In other words, he painted his memories and sought to recapture the emotions they had awakened in him at the time. These were defining memories, or they became such when he painted them; they were the basis of his understanding of himself, in them he could seek out what had made him who he was. Memories have this function for all of us. Without memories the thoughts and experiences we have and the feelings we experience would be as new every time, and our self would not have the force to maintain itself but would dissolve into the moment, would be boundless and unfathomable. This tells us that the self is something beyond our thoughts and emotions, perhaps merely a perspective on them.

That processes occurring in the brain can be fixed must at some point during the beginnings of life have come about through a practical need, so that the methods for staying alive, that is, the obeying of inherited drives, didn't have to be reinvented each time. What characterises human beings is that everything which is experienced can in principle be fixed, so that the mass of elements against which the self views its thoughts and emotions becomes so overwhelming that the self becomes the primary thing, in other words the experience of existing, while maintaining this existence becomes secondary.

In the earliest art we know of, cave paintings some 40,000 years old, it is as if the two levels, experience and the maintaining of existence, are found side by side. The motifs are animals, around which early men's lives must have been centred, since they lived off hunting, and it may well be that painting pictures of them meant conjuring them up, but what remains for us is the existential surplus, the joy and wonder that the animals exist, the manifest feeling of belonging with them, which the paintings not only show but also intensify because through the paintings the animals are drawn into the notional world of human beings. This notional world stands in the same relation to the external world as the self does in relation to the inner world: it prevents us from vanishing into it.

Both the self and the notional world are immaterial entities, they don't exist in the same way elements of physical reality do, but represent a perspective on them, and in a certain sense it may be meaningful to call them fictions. But even though we understand the self through stories and are unable to represent it through anything else (Freud's story about the self being the best known), in itself it forms no story, in itself it has no form. The inner world itself is unconveyed, that is its nature. The conveying of it, that is, the fiction or the story, is our way of understanding the self.

Munch's ambition was to paint the story about the self, and the method he found was stylised and dream-like representations of inner experiences which were unified enough and lay close enough to known stories or archetypes to be decoded and understood. He removed everything specific and detailed, allowing only the unspecified sweep of memory to remain around the essential, which emerged with the force of a sudden and terrible memory.

But what is the self beyond the story? One way of seeing it is as a place that is continually becoming, where what is happening is continually merging with what has happened in ways and forms determined by previous experiences more or less powerful and decisive, but regardless of how rigid they might become eventually, there will still be movement, albeit along the same channels. The self is a work in progress, it understands itself through its memories but lives its life between them, in bits and pieces, in the present and in the past, in thoughts and emotions. And that is my story about the inner: something chaotic that one seeks to control through habits and experiences, sketch-like, unfinished, raw and unrefined.

For the third exhibition room, following the harmonious first room filled with people and the deserted second room, I therefore chose fragmented, unfinished and rough pictures: an old man with a mask-like face sitting with a young girl on his lap; the famous jealousy motif reduced to its very essence; the faces of a man and a woman in the background with a man's face in the foreground; a woman's back; a cascade of blood; a standing man and a seated woman in a picture that radiates unease and aggression; a triptych with twisted bodies; people in a death room more drawn than painted, in strong reds and greens; a seated woman with a mask on the floor in a painting so damaged that it appears to be something from antiquity, a wall in Pompeii. Everything is Munch, everything comes from him, and everything can be incorporated within the inner structures that the paintings in the Frieze of Life established, while at the same time this unity is purely notional.

Moving on from this room one then enters the last one, which has only pictures from the external world, in the form of a row of full-length portraits along one wall, along the others etchings, lithographs and woodcuts of faces. All were of people Munch had met and related to. Some of them he had loved, some he had feared, some had been drinking companions, others he had discussed art with or sold pictures to. But most importantly they were all people he had seen. For that too was a distinguishing feature of Munch and his character as a painter, how open he was to other people, not necessarily to their inner world, but to their aura. The portraits often live in the tension between the momentary impression and what it tells us about the character, and they differ from his self-portraits, which to a greater extent seem founded on something lasting, they are weightier and less fleeting than the portraits. The self-portraits show a human being as he is, while in the portraits one can easily imagine that the portrayed, as soon as they are out of sight and by themselves, will show something very different. Some of the pictures have an aura almost like that of real people, especially, to my mind, the portrait of Aase Nørregaard, who is incomparably alive. That he was close to her is obvious, he paints her as she is to him, and we can see the effect she has on him. Place the portrait of Aase next to *The Scream*, and you see not only the span of Munch's emotions but also of a life.

*

Its storage space must be the Munch Museum's inner sanctum, that is where the main body of the collection is found, more than a thousand paintings that were in Munch's possession when he died and which he willed to the Municipality of Oslo, in other words those paintings he didn't sell and the versions of well-known paintings which he painted again in order to have after he had sold the originals. Time-wise they span the decades from the 1870s to the 1940s. The selection of paintings in this large collection was in a sense dictated by the art market, since the pictures which museums and art dealers in Munch's time were interested in and acquired are not part of it. The most significant Munch collection in the world belongs to the Norwegian National Museum, it comprises almost exclusively pictures now considered masterpieces, bought at the beginning of the twentieth century by its then director Jens Thiis. The Munch Museum's collection is vastly larger and much more interesting, since it covers every epoch, track and sidetrack in his artistic career, but it is also much more difficult to evaluate in terms of quality, since such a large part of it consists of uncanonical works, and it contains pictures that have never been shown, including sloppy or trifling works, complete failures, first attempts and experiments.

Munch kept everything; even the heavy stones he used to

print lithographs, which it would have been natural to reuse or throw away, he dragged home with him from Europe and saved. Since Munch was such a careless painter, often uninterested in finishing his canvases, it can be difficult to say what status he himself assigned to his pictures, whether he considered them finished works, sketches or failures. One possible way of evaluating the collection is to say that it contains all his less successful works, in other words, one considers the pictures he sold his most successful. At the same time we know that Munch sold his work reluctantly, he called his pictures his 'children', and it is difficult to know how he judged the pictures that weren't canonised in his lifetime.

The storage space resembles above all a bomb shelter, its walls, floor and ceiling made of concrete and the door of solid iron, but unlike a bomb shelter it has a high ceiling, perhaps five metres, and along the entire length of one of the walls there are closely spaced partitions reaching to about the middle of the room. There are pictures hanging on both sides of them, but the partitions are so close together, almost like the filing jackets in a filing cabinet, that one cannot see the pictures until they are pulled out into the room. Only the conservators are allowed to touch them, so there we stood, Kari Brandtzæg and I, looking on as a conservator wearing white gloves slowly pulled out one of the enormous partitions, and picture after picture appeared. They were not in chronological order, and it was impossible to predict which pictures would emerge. It was as if they were naked, it occurred to me, or unprotected. When exhibited in a museum each picture is hung in accordance with a carefully thought-out system, covered with glass and furnished with a plaque printed with the title and date and perhaps also an interpretative or contextual comment. These pictures seemed to hang just anyhow, few of them were glazed, and striking masterpieces hung side by side with the most unassuming sketches, wild experiments hung next to conventional landscapes, pictures from the 1880s alongside pictures from the 1930s, portraits and self-portraits with pictures of interiors, construction sites, city streets, shorelines, smooth rocky slopes, copses, fields, gardens. Some paintings were impressionistic, some were dark and as heavily glowing as Rembrandt's, some were naturalistic, some symbolistic, some almost abstract.

To see all these paintings, and in this way, filled me with excitement, something febrile and boundless, for a whole life lay behind them filled with intensity, suffering, joy and creative force, which I had never before been so close to, and a whole epoch, which also seemed strangely present.

We looked at the pictures I wanted to include in the exhibition, occasionally Kari directed my attention to some I hadn't noticed or hadn't thought would fit in, we included some and rejected others, and it was a difficult task, since the criteria were unclear. A picture might fit thematically in a given room and yet I felt there was something about it I didn't like, it didn't do anything for me or it was banal, like the painting of a woman and hands reaching for her body and wanting to touch her, which qualified for the inner room, where gender was perhaps the most important factor, but which didn't match my notion of quality, while at the same time it was undoubtedly Munch and represented his notion. So was I trying to 'save' him from himself? Was I creating an image of him which didn't actually fit him, but rather me – and if so, with what right? Could I place myself 'above' Munch and direct his pictures into something which didn't really accord with his view of reality? And then there were pictures I intuitively didn't like but included anyway because they fitted the criteria, that is, they weren't typical of Munch yet could be subsumed under one of the four themes, and because I felt I didn't have a right to gainsay him – since he had painted them, surely they had to be good?

When I read Stian Grøgaard's book, the selection had already been made, in principle the exhibition was finished. Only then did I realise how naive I had been, simply snatching up pictures, for what Grøgaard did, which was rather unusual in the literature about Munch, was to judge the painterly quality of individual works in a way I perceived as being if not purely objective then at least clear-sighted and convincing.

Would the pictures I had selected withstand such an objective, critical, pre-canonical gaze? I noticed that Grøgaard called many of the pictures in the Munch Museum's collection 'basement drudges', and I was seized by a bottomless anxiety: had I selected all the poor paintings by Munch based on an underlying notion that they were good because Munch had painted them?

At about the same time I sent an email to David Hockney – his knowledge of painting is enormous, and I thought it would be a good idea to invite him to an onstage conversation about Munch in connection with the exhibition opening. I received a nice reply, he wrote that he had several major exhibitions during the coming year and that his hearing was almost gone, but that he was interested in Munch and didn't rule out coming. I sent him the list of works and the virtual exhibition, and then I didn't hear from him again.

Did he fail to reply because the pictures were so weak? He, if anyone, would be qualified to judge them, I didn't know anyone who could speak better or more interestingly and insightfully about painting in all its aspects than Hockney.

Why hadn't I thought of this before? Why hadn't I chosen some of the masterpieces, those that were as safe as the bank in terms of quality, why, oh why this endless row of sketch-like paintings lacking any charge?

It was at about this time that I sent Grøgaard an email asking if he might be willing to be interviewed about Munch for this book. He was, and I suggested that we meet in the basement storage space and look at pictures together.

*

Slim, dressed in black, with sharp features I thought of as somewhat 1930s-ish and greying, combed-back hair, Stian Grøgaard stood next to me in the storage space a few weeks later. His eyes reminded me vaguely of Paul Auster's, something about the faintly pouch-like wrinkles beneath them, perhaps, while his gaze was at once friendly and sharp.

– We don't have any plan, I told the gloved conservator who had given me a half-questioning, half-encouraging look. – There are no particular pictures we want to look at. When I was here the first time, you just pulled pictures out, so one didn't know what was coming.

– Is there a chronology here? Grøgaard said. – Is it thematic?

– It's partly thematic, and partly chronological, but then suddenly it jumps again, the conservator said.

– OK, he said.

– One of the most exciting things I have experienced in my professional life was coming here to look at pictures, I said. – Not knowing what would come next. All kinds of strange stuff appeared.

– Actually I've never been here before, Grøgaard said. – And I haven't pulled anything out. I've only been to the library here when I've been working on Munch.

– Very few people are allowed down here, the conservator said as she slowly pulled out one of the partitions with pictures, most of them drawings or half-painted sketches.

– These are probably sketches he made while he was working on *History*, he said. – And they may have been made in Kragerø, where I come from.

– You've painted yourself, haven't you?

– I studied at the art academy and was a professional painter for a few years. And then I married a painter, and one of us had to find paid employment, so I became a teacher. But I also have a philosophy degree. So it's kind of a combination. Philosophers love concepts, and I try to enter Munch's universe armed with a few concepts that help one see it a little clearer. But of course I do bring with me some technical and practical competence from my training as a painter. I would sit copying in the National Gallery sometimes, including early Munch paintings. I was actually born in the place where Munch painted the sunrise! On the hill where he stood, and where he painted the portrait of Christian Gierløff. Right across from there is where I grew up. Ten metres away.

– One of the things you wrote in your book which made the greatest impression on me, which I believe is entirely true and which must have come from an actual experience, is what you say about style. That style is a way of controlling information. I have never seen this expressed anywhere else. But in that case, what is it like to copy Munch? Since then you are actually entering the same process and facing the same problems, except that they have already been solved?

– Yes, then you are coming to a sort of ready-made process. But a picture contains enormous amounts of information. In the old days one copied plaster or marble statues to learn how to draw, because monochrome sculptures were so well suited for analysing the play of light and shadow. And then one went over to drawing live models. So I have some of that old-fashioned training. I'm not sure I actually learned anything from it, but you become very familiar with the paintings!

We moved around to the other side of the partition.

– More sketches, I said. Grøgaard moved up close to the pictures and traced the contours of one of them in the air with his hand.

– This is a painter who made 1,789 paintings. In addition to drawings and graphic works and prints. You can almost *see* the pace at which the paintings were made. How quickly they were painted.

– What you said, that they would paint from plaster sculptures and paintings and models in order to learn technique, is interesting in Munch's case. You write that it had to do with processing information and acquiring methods for this. And that Munch ran into difficulties with that when he painted *The Sick Child*. Why was that, do you think? What was it that hindered him, why didn't he have it in him – and why just him? Why did he of all people encounter this difficulty?

– It is said about the architecture of Vienna, and its cultural life as a whole, that around the turn of the century there was a *panic of style*. If one considers the whole span from art nouveau to its opposite, functionalism, there was a desperate search going on for a kind of overarching form. And it hit Munch smack in the face as a young student at the joint studio Pultosten. His early years are marked by this kind of panic of style.

– Just him, or everyone?

– Especially him. Some had the patience required to become even more outré naturalists than Christian Krohg and Frits Thaulow, who would come to Pultosten and correct their work. In Gustav Wentzel and Kalle Løchen, for example, who belonged to the same milieu as Munch, one can see that they took pleasure in detail. Wentzel in particular was consistently naturalistic, he seemed to outdo the previous generation of naturalists with details and a kind of *anti*-composition. But Munch simply lacks the will for that, he is *lazier* than them, in a way. He would rather learn from Christian Krohg's somewhat more impressionistic way of working. And then he has a problem. He can't simply repeat Krohg's naturalism or realism, it doesn't come as easily to him, and he doesn't go in the direction of a highly detailed style, clamping on to the motif and taking in an enormous amount of information the way Wentzel does. So what does he do? *The Sick Child* is an example of this despair. For in addition to observing a model taking the place of his sister, and Aunt Karen in Aunt Karen's place from the time when Sophie died – she died in 1878, and he began painting *The*

Sick Child in 1885 – he is also recreating that experience, what the English call re-enacting. What he wants to do is to create a remembered image. Somewhere around there is where things begin to happen. He wants to bring forth an emotion and to observe it at the same time. You might say that in *The Sick Child* there is a conflict of aesthetics. You have an aesthetics of observation, and you have a kind of aesthetics of remembering.

– Do you think Munch himself was aware of the conflict in that way? Or do you think he was just trying to do something but didn't know what it was?

– I don't think he was aware of it in that way, but I do think he was ambitious, and he wanted to expand Krohg and Thaulow's painterly programme with remembering. After all, it was in the air. They were probably more *au courant* than we think! Symbolism was under way internationally, there was Arnhold Böcklin in Switzerland, for example, who painted memory paintings with a few minor observations which make them look as if they had been seen, as in *Isle of the Dead, Die Toteninsel* (1880–6). It is skilfully painted, but it is also a kind of memory or dream painting, a picture that isn't observed. So it was in the air. From Munch's writings it isn't easy to determine how much he knew about French or German Symbolism, for example, but they probably knew something, and Krohg was relatively well informed. But a more philosophical point is that two styles or two views of painting collide in *The Sick Child*. And it is interesting to note that he didn't repeat the solution he found in that painting later. That painting didn't become Edvard Munch. But it could have! Apparently Hans Jæger told him that he mustn't paint any more pictures like that. But I also think it's possible that he didn't go back to it because the picture itself became traumatic for him. He lost his sister, and he worked on that painting for a whole year. That tells us something.

– What happens to his painting after *The Sick Child*?

– He goes towards the opposite extreme. While he begins his career with close observation, where things happen as the painting is under way and he is almost passive in the painting process, keeping uncorrected lucky accidents which occur on the canvas as he paints, during the 1890s he becomes an intention-driven, calculating painter, for whom observation is no longer essential. He practically fantasises his way into the painting. You might say that he has become a kind of conceptual painter, he more or less settles on an iconography, a dramatic solution to a situation, and paints it into the picture without necessarily needing a model as he paints. It is as if after 1890 he is governed by a certain iconography. And that is what he has become known for.

– If he is painting a shoe, for instance, he does it in the same way everywhere, as if it is already finished before he begins to paint?

– Yes.

– That's like with icon paintings, isn't it?

– You could well say that, it is something like that. His work is full of mannerisms. One of his mannerisms is the wavy lines. They appeared before he had arrived at a Symbolist conviction. As early as 1887–8 the curved lines are there, and the gentle rounding of the figures. Often the drawing is what I would call sloppy. I wonder if he himself was aware of it? At drawing school he had been taught that there should be a variation of lines, a mixture of straight and curved lines, but he keeps giving in to these curves. It is almost as if there is a regression. In my book I talk about deskilling, and in his mannerist way of drawing there would seem to be a willed deskilling.

– But couldn't that also be a sign of great strength and not just sloppiness? That he goes against what he knows? Would you say that Munch was a strong painter?

– Well, he was an excellent draughtsman, in his paintings he comes across as a draughtsman. As a draughtsman he is fairly dry, but there is something drawn about his paintings. And that may be one of the reasons why his position within the history of modernism is a bit dubious. In the narrow history of abstraction from Cézanne, Matisse, Picasso and onwards.

– His pictures from the 1890s were very successful, they made his name. Why do you think he stopped painting that way, why did he abandon that project?

– Well, he was sensitive to ideological shifts, and by around the year 1900 Symbolism was a dead horse. In 1902–3 he understands that piling up dramatic and literary items in his paintings is not what he ought to be doing. You can see this in *Girls on the Bridge*, for example, it has some of the same sinuous style, but it's just an ordinary everyday situation, a Sunday on the pier in Åsgårdstrand. So you might say he is emptied of his own dramaticism around 1900.

– From your point of view, does that make his pictures better or weaker?

– I must say that I admire *The Scream*, for one would think it really couldn't work, and *Melancholy* and *Despair* and others, they are fantastic, but that hasn't been my main interest in Munch. I think his skill at observation, and for that matter his way of negotiating with observation when it comes to style, is very interesting. What he starts to do after 1900 is to produce paintings based more on observation. One might say that Symbolism consists of solemn or grandiose motifs painted in a careful or pusillanimous way. That is true of Gustave Moreau and Böcklin, for example. And one could say that expressionism is trivial motifs painted in a wild way. What is striking about Munch, and what makes him special, is that he paints solemn motifs, like *The Scream* and *Despair* and *Melancholy*, in a wild way. He stands midway between the two schools. So even though it appears calculated, this iconography, there is something rough and precarious about the way he works. And this to me makes him always interesting. But then expressionism comes along right after the turn of the century, and Munch too moves on to more trivial motifs, like the expressionists in France and Germany. It is difficult to say which way the influence went, in other words what he saw. But he was probably influenced by the fauvists, and they were probably not influenced by him, although some Munch experts have concluded that Matisse may have been looking over Munch's shoulder in the 1890s and so on, but I don't really think so.

– But if he returned to a way of painting that was more based on observation, what happened then to the problems he ran into with *The Sick Child*? Did he carry the idea of mannerism, the idea of simplification, with him, is that what enabled him to go back there, for it seems as if the problem no longer existed for him?

– He has figured out how he wants to do things, so in a way one might say that after 1900 he changes his theme but sticks to his way of working. He straightens out his lines a little, he doesn't have the waviness to the same extent, but he never loses it entirely.

In his book on Munch Grøgaard is particularly interested in a few pictures that Munch painted when he had his studio at Pultosten in the early 1880s together with other young artists in Kristiania. These are portraits, Munch himself called them 'heads', glowing heavily against a black or brown background, and there is something classical, almost Rembrandtesque about them.

When the conservator pulled out the next partition, we were faced with one of them. A young man with a reddish moustache, a ruddy face, red-brown hair, blue, somewhat evasive eyes.

– This is a very early picture, isn't it? I said. – Munch wasn't very old when he did this, was he?

– No. And I think I can see that Krohg has been here and made some corrections . . .

– It's a painting from Pultosten?

– It's a painting from Pultosten. He has painted Andreas Singdahlsen, a colleague of his. And part of the mystery of Munch is that he – more so than Krohg and Thaulow, really – has this ability to find a grand, sculptural form in the heads he paints. And I have wondered, where did it come from? For Thaulow's naturalism is more even, sort of all over in the details, while with Munch there is something almost old-fashioned, baroquely insistent about the heads he paints. This is one of them. There are better ones that he made at around the same time, but this one is all right.

– I've always thought Munch was such an incredibly talented painter; looking at his early pictures, I've thought, bloody hell, he was just eighteen or twenty, but then I read your book and you say no, actually he was technically *limited*, even compared to other young painters who were his contemporaries.

– What we need to remember is that the great unlearning in the history of European painting was naturalism. That's when the entire tradition of studio painting was thrown overboard. You had to remove the shoe polish, as Munch put it. With regard to tradition, open-air painting and naturalism was one huge Delete button. The repertoire of craftsmanlike skill is replaced by the repertoire of observation. In a way, Munch is a part of this enormous renovation of the history of painting. He was a very skilled draughtsman, but there were certainly others at Pultosten who had a greater repertoire than he did.

– But no one else at Pultosten could have made this? I said, pointing to the picture hanging next to the portrait of Singdahlsen. It depicted the Polish writer Stanislaw Przybyszewski and was radically different in style, much flatter, almost entirely without depth, less painted than drawn.

– No, that's true, Grøgaard said. – This is from his time in Berlin, and there Munch learned to appreciate one thing, and that was the technique of casein tempera painting, which produces a matt finish and a mural effect. He hadn't come across that before. What he had done before that was oil painting. At times you can see how his oils get a chalky colour. This is probably just a sketch he has abandoned, but . . . At times the whites become milky, he can't quite get the colour to chime, and that is what you see here.

– Exactly.

– Often his light and shadow get a little grubby, but

tempera allows him to paint more directly, it dries quickly, and this lets him think more decoratively. And what Munch learns around the 1890s is that painting must serve a decorative function, not merely a referential or a documentary function.

– Singdahlsen's head is more sculptural, Przybyszewski's is more flat, but still incredibly better, isn't it?

Why on earth did I say that? Intuitively I valued the sculptural and Rembrandtesque classic portrait higher than the sketch-like one, so why was I now saying the opposite? Presumably because I knew this was the ruling consensus, that the figurative Munch was much weaker and less interesting than the later, more direct and simplified Munch, and that there he captured the people, whereas in the earlier portraits, which were also exercises, he built people up. Since Grøgaard was a professor of art theory and an expert on Munch, I wanted to show him that I too knew a thing or two about Munch, that I saw straight through convention to what was really good.

But Grøgaard disagreed, so I was left looking doubly stupid, as I gazed at the portraits.

– I quite like it when he manages to combine naturalistic observation with a form of abstract understanding of volume, he said. – I have been very interested in baroque portraiture precisely because it combines observation with an insistence on volume. But these are two extremes.

– Yes, it was nice to see them next to each other, they reveal such an enormous change in a short time. We can go behind here and see . . . Here is another portrait from about the same time . . .

– Yes, that must be Aunt Karen, I suppose. That one is rather less successful.

Oh no! This was one of the few pictures from that period which I had selected for the exhibition. And now he thought it unsuccessful? Maybe it was? Wasn't there something about the mouth and the area around it that was poor? But the colours were nice, weren't they? Or not?

– To me, the first really good portrait he made was of his sister Laura, Grøgaard continued, wholly oblivious of my inner panic, and he pointed to another picture which I had never noticed before. – It was made in 1881, I think, which is the year before Munch joins Pultosten. In a sense he is already on his way, and he has probably seen some art in the high romantic mode here – for this isn't bad, really, a little high-toned perhaps, but I find it very sensitive and nice.

– 'High-toned', what does that mean?

– It isn't altogether chalky, but the articulation of space in the face is possibly a little dead. It seems a little overexposed, somehow. A little too much light. But it's a fine picture.

– Should we move to the next one? This is going to take a long time, there's so much to talk about!

The conservator pushed the partition slowly back again, and just as slowly pulled out a new one further down.

– How did you relate to Munch when you were still painting? I asked as we waited. – As an historical figure, or as someone who had found solutions to problems that were still relevant?

– Well, I'm from the countryside, from an environment that is in many ways rather old-fashioned, dominated by neo-romanticism, so I actually viewed Munch as a modern painter. I was a hundred years too late! It has struck me that that was one of the reasons I stopped painting. This is modern enough for me.

A version of *Death in the Sickroom* glided out in front of us.

– This is like theatre, almost, I said. – Drama. How did Munch's pictorial world relate to that?

– Well, this is the scene from *The Sick Child*, but here the perspective has been moved outwards. Instead of a close-up of a dying child, the main thing here is the grief of the people standing around. It was made during his time in Berlin, I think, and whereas *The Sick Child* is thickly and pastosely painted, you can see here that he has learned how to apply paint thinly and to lay down surfaces. This is actually a decorative representation, although it is rather heavy. The green wall, the reddish-yellow floor, and then you have the figures grouped together, so that the format is divided up efficiently.

– Was this something found in Europe at the same time, I mean the theatricality, that way of conceiving of paintings?

– Yes, I think you'll find it in both German and French Symbolism, Gustave Moreau and Odilon Redon and a few others who got there before Munch. But this way of dividing the picture up into large surfaces one might say is J. F. Willumsen's interpretation of Paul Gauguin, which may have influenced Munch. Willumsen understood the significance of Gauguin quite early.

– Imagine that this was the only picture of Munch that existed, how do you think Munch would have been viewed then?

– Then he would have been an example of a Symbolist painter, a post-naturalist, a non-naturalist painter, a little behind what is going on in Europe. But it would still have been linked to his biography, I think.

– You wouldn't have considered it original or innovative?

– Well . . . Munch is easy to recognise, of course. He has

a strong style. All significant artists have a strong style. So I think I might have said something like what you said a while ago, that we're dealing with a tough painter here. There's will here, he takes a risk by working in this way. It has to do with his self-image, I think he felt he was *entitled* to do these wild things. Many of the other painters at Pultosten came from the countryside, they were – I almost said – millers' sons, who had the idea of becoming painters so they wouldn't have to carry fifty-kilo sacks of flour. A humble lad like Skredsvig, for example, who was so happy to be able to *paint*, right, to sit there and fiddle with his brushes. You can sense that Munch is from the cultured bourgeoisie and has ambitions on his own and his family's behalf. His uncle was P. A. Munch, after all, the great historian. Munch visits Rome in 1927 and paints his uncle's tombstone in the non-Catholic graveyard there. So this is also an expression of family feeling. One has to keep this in mind about Munch, that he felt representative.

A new partition with pictures came gliding out. And my spirits lifted, for one of them was the portrait of Aase Nørregaard, which was perhaps the best of all the full-length portraits that were going to be in the exhibition. She is painted wearing a blue dress, standing with one closed hand lifted to her waist, the other hand down along her side, against a green and greenish-yellow background, with a beaming face, and something about the figure makes it seem as if it is on its way out of the painting.

– Aase Nørregaard was the love he never dared, Grøgaard said. – She was a friend of his, and she married Harald Nørregaard, who invested in paintings by Munch early on. She died young, barely forty, and it affected Munch deeply. There is something about the repetition of losses – his mother, his sister, his father, his brother. But also that there was no conflict between them, since they had never been lovers. I think he felt that she was a woman who understood and respected him. Munch is strangely selective in his empathy, by the way. Sometimes he is incredibly considerate, at other times strikingly indifferent towards others.

– But what would you say of this picture in purely painterly terms?

– Well, this is the so-called 'bodyguard format', two by one metre, which he liked and painted over many years. I think the turpentine-diluted greenery is a little hollow, there is something not entirely convincing about the green background. And the dress could have been given more shape, I think he gets a little lost with all his flecking. He's a little lazy, he gives up quickly. He makes a start, and then he can't be bothered any more. So the painting lacks *wholeness*. But the face is *always* . . . almost always, interesting. He is a great portraitist, no doubt about it.

– Shall we look at another one?

– Sure.

A new partition came gliding out in front of us, full of late pictures, most of them with garden motifs.

– I've always liked this one a lot, Grøgaard said, pointing to one of the pictures from the Linde Frieze, *Girls Watering Flowers*, which was going to be in the exhibition. – Because he is caught up in the colours. The greenery holds its own as form everywhere, and the red figure too. It's a wonderful picture. All the colours suit it – yellow hat, green background, red shirt – and it is so splendidly drawn: bang, and it's done. In a couple of hours, probably. He painted that potted plant a number of times, with the heavy leaves, but when he does the moist green with a drawing like this, it's solid. The painting reminds one a little of the French fauvism of the day, perhaps.

– What about these? I said, nodding towards some pictures of the apple orchard at Ekely, including one with a woman and a man in front of an apple tree, and one of a tree heavily laden with apples in front of his studio. – All of them are going to be in the exhibition.

– This picture here is too blue and green. He lacks something to temper the image. And this one here, in blue and green, it's too purple. But *here* I think he's accomplished a good balance. And then I ask myself whether this is what he was trying to accomplish, or whether he just didn't give a damn. Is he trying to create an interesting temperature in the picture, or does he simply not care, is he just thinking of the Adam and Eve motif? It's hard to tell! He said something interesting once about Ludvig Karsten: 'Karsten manages something with colour that I can never do. But I have more under my waistcoat!' On the other hand Munch often has more interesting combinations than Karsten, who is often a little too sweet-toned, often too pleasing in his use of colour. Whereas Munch sometimes succeeds with unpleasant colours, which together produce an interesting effect. You find the same thing in Matisse. Sophisticated, unharmonious things which at times fit very well together.

– But what do you think he was after? OK, so he's in his garden, and he's going to paint an apple tree. But what's driving him to do this?

– I think he is a typical painter fascinated by observation, he sees the world around him and it is full of interesting things, an apple tree or a dog or whatever, and then he stands there working at it, and then the main thing is the battle between what he sees and what he paints. That somewhat sweeping, grand quality he has which means that on the one hand he is in control of the painting, on the other hand he is actually documenting his observations. He is a confident painter who needs to test his confidence against new observations. And sometimes the result is like this, sometimes it's like that. I don't think he's walking around with a ruler in hand, thinking, he's not the kind of painter who stands contemplating the picture afterwards saying, hm, I need to add a little more red here.

– But do you think he himself thought in terms of what you've been saying, OK, there's something wrong about the colour here, it's a little flat or dead, and in that case why didn't he start again and paint it *better*?

– Yes, he should have been able to draw out something that could withstand all that blue-green, instead everything is just swept together into a big blue-green heap. I think there's rather too much greenery in many of his late pictures. And that is a sign he is letting himself be governed by observation to a great extent. But that he could stand out there in the garden and let it be *that* blue-green, how could he be so unaware? To just let himself be overpowered by an observation in that way! I think I would have tried to resist all that greenery somewhat, anyhow. In this I am a typical bourgeois, for he's probably thinking, *It doesn't matter!* At some point or other it just doesn't matter!

– This is very interesting because it has to do with what quality is, doesn't it?

While we spoke we had moved away from the garden

pictures to the paintings of the elm forest. Munch painted fifteen or twenty of them in the mid-1920s, more than almost any other motif.

– Yes, Grøgaard said, looking up at the enormous twisted tree trunks in front of us. – And the big question about the older Munch, from 1917 onwards, is what does he want? What is he up to? What are his ambitions for painting?

– This is something he very often succeeds with, Grøgaard said and let his finger trace one of the twisted trees in the air. – The trunks. And the way he divides it up. Sometimes what he does feels grand and majestic, it has what the English call scale. A dimension. We feel a certain solemnity even in a small format owing to the way he has divided it up. At other times it just doesn't work, nothing comes of it, it just fizzles out. And then you think, Doesn't it mean anything to him? But at the same time I wonder if I'm applying the wrong scale. To measure this against? His late work?

– Could one imagine something we might call 'pure painting'? That he simply paints, and that's all there is to it? And if so, what is the result? The quality declines, the individual pictures lose their force, the iconography vanishes, and then the value is lost too. Or is it the other way round, that something else comes into being?

– I think perhaps that should be our starting point, that something else comes into being. That one doesn't depict Munch as someone who has lost interest, in a way, someone who paints simply because he doesn't know how to do anything else. Let's say that is what he's after here. It must be that. How are we to understand it? In a way it is a lame comparison, but you have Søren Kierkegaard's three stages, which you could also divide Munch's *oeuvre* into. You have the aesthetic stage, that's the naturalist who made *The Sick Child*. You have the ethical stage, that's the symbolist who painted *The Scream* and *Melancholy*. The religious stage would then be the artist who after the turn of the century develops a new observation-based painting using trivial motifs. But what is religious about it? Apparently nothing. But let's think . . . Could it be painting as a kind of cosmological practice? Tending to the world? You're out there looking, you have the talent for it, you have the required sensitivity, and you deal only with your own perception in a simple, de-ideologised, almost postmodern or post-religious way. I don't really know, it's easy to invest too much in these concepts, but perhaps they do after all have something to say about this. A form of cosmology or caretaking. He tends to his immediate world. And he practises painting as only he knows how.

*

Although one gets closer to Munch's artistic practice in the Munch Museum's storage rooms than perhaps anywhere else, since the paintings there have not been selected or curated but comprise all the pictures Munch had around him at the time of his death, and in that way represent some of the force and the chaos he worked within, and some of the arbitrariness and processuality, nevertheless more than seventy years have passed since they were in circulation, so more than anything else they are elements of a sort of painterly mausoleum, from when time stopped and work on them ceased. Since then many new generations of artists have been active in a world which has changed rather drastically, not least in relation to the visual.

How do artists working now view Munch's practice? How relevant are his pictures to them?

There are probably as many answers to that question as there are artists. One artist I have been most curious about in this respect is Vanessa Baird. Her pictures have both a wildness and a will to break free of visual expectations which make me think there is a kinship with Munch, if not directly and specifically then at least indirectly, through a fundamental attitude to what it is to paint, what painting should do.

There is something deeply unpredictable about Vanessa Baird's art, her pictures are powerfully emotive, they are often disturbing and discomfiting, sometimes beautiful but always intense, and it is as if many of them manage to reach a place or a point from which significance spreads outwards in waves, becoming greater than themselves in the way a myth can be, or an allegory. But allegory sounds harmless, allegory sounds like a non-committal story about something which is also something else, and Baird's pictures are neither non-committal nor harmless. One such point of expansive signification is all the papers or documents falling through the various motifs in her work *Light disappears as soon as we close our eyes*, we immediately understand what they are, for we have seen public buildings collapse following terror attacks, and yet we have never seen it like this, taken out of context and inserted into other situations and landscapes, where it has retained its striking visual force from the catastrophe but is also seen afresh, open to new interpretations, where the fact that it is a shared visual experience, a part of the collective unconscious, something that floods through us all, becomes visible, so that it is detached from its original context and becomes a sign.

Several of her pictures take their motifs from fairy tales, referring to folk notions but as it were turning them inside out, uncompromising in their grotesque corporeality, which in turn has to do with something of the same, the collective myths and images that exist above us, if not beautifying then harmless, whereas what is within us, or what we exist in, is acute in a whole other way. She has made a series of pictures of drowning people, they exist in that same span between ourselves and the stories and images we relate to and which serve to maintain a distance, a distance which Baird's pictures alternately thematise and breach. She has made many pictures of animals, badgers and foxes, where the logic of fairy tales – animals who are like people but also always animals – brings human nature into play. In one striking image a badger snuffles the crotch of a reclining girl. Baird's pictures are often large, while the motifs can be small, the surface of the picture swarming with details, and the tension between the two levels echoes that between the overarching and the acute.

What do her pictures have to do with Munch?

If one considers his paintings from the 1890s, the answer is not very much, for Baird punctures any attempt at solemnity and wholeness. But Baird has also painted landscapes so radically simplified that they seem close to children's drawings, while at the same time the atmosphere and the colour harmony remain more or less intact, and it feels as if she has taken Munch's landscapes down a level. And the sketchiness, the effort to reach a place that whirls up significance without the painterly or visual perfection of this place mattering in the slightest, this too has something in common with Munch, as I see it.

A couple of years ago I asked her to contribute some illustrations to a book I had written, *Autumn*. She said yes, and after a while during which nothing happened I suddenly received a flood of pictures. One of them was a classic madonna with child, where the madonna's face was blotted out by something that looked like faeces. That became the back cover of the book and was a reality check for me while I wrote it, for if the beauty of the iconic image of mother and child is true, and if the world is at times unbearably beautiful, the opposite is also always the case.

I met Vanessa Baird at a restaurant in Oslo just before Christmas, together with Kari Brandtzæg. They already knew each other, Kari had included several of Vanessa's pictures in exhibitions she had curated. I was a little nervous, since I had heard that she could be difficult, which is perhaps simply another word for uncompromising, but not necessarily, and I also hadn't made a plan or thought out any questions beforehand. That whole day I had spent sitting in Villa Stenersen, the functionalist house that belonged to Munch's patron, helper and eventual biographer, Rolf Stenersen, talking about Munch with Joachim Trier for a film his brother Emil was making. We had talked about the really big emotions and about the existential foundations of art, and after a few seconds at the same table as Vanessa Baird it became apparent that she was unlikely to do the same. She gave me a book she had made, containing self-portraits, where her face, always recognisable, swelled, became distorted, bloated and ugly in wild and ever-changing ways. She has an illness which means that she has to be hospitalised from time to time, and which can make her face bloated – whether this is caused by the medication or the illness I didn't quite catch – but the suffering in those pictures didn't have to do with the soul or with existence, or it did, of course, but not in any solemn way, it was concrete and physical, and the pictures related to it with irony and humour, while at the same time the pain was always present in them too. The pictures appeared to have been made by an anti-myth mythomaniac. Someone who was totally down to earth, but allowed the down-to-earthness to escalate.

She had come into the crowded little fish restaurant downtown, which was full of people attending Christmas parties, sat down and pushed the book into my hands. After leafing through it for a while, I switched on the recorder on my mobile and asked her a hesitant and half-apologetic question about her relation to Munch.

– Munch is a subject everyone knows something about, she said. – Everyone knows his pictures so well, and you feel it so strongly when you look at them, but it's difficult to say anything about them because the stuff he makes is all emotion. And it's embarrassing to talk about. But easy to recognise. There isn't much more to say about it than that he's good at that particular thing, is there? Even when he paints hands that look like a pile of twigs. For most of his pictures have a lot of weaknesses. And then there are some which are very well articulated. But they don't need any explanation. When he paints someone who is dying, they are so awfully dead, because the people standing next to them are so red in the face. And you feel a kind of exhaustion. Because it's so embarrassing.

– What is embarrassing?

– To say it. You see the pictures, you recognise the

feeling, and that's it, really. *Jealousy* is a pretty intense picture, but all it really consists of, is that everyone recognises it. So what are you supposed to say? Like, these are good pictures?

– I brought the list of works for the exhibition, if you want to have a look at them, Kari said. Vanessa nodded, and Kari placed a folder with the pictures on the table in front of her, which she flipped through from time to time while she talked.

– Since I live in Oslo, I've been to the Munch Museum a lot, she said. – I've seen many of the exhibitions where they try to give a new twist to it by juxtaposing Munch with other artists, but the straight exhibitions are much better, then you can relate to what you're seeing, and then it becomes clear or visible what he's doing. Many of his pictures aren't very good, and it doesn't matter. It allows one to appreciate one's own excellence now and again, right. Walking around looking and finding all these feeble paintings he hasn't succeeded with. It makes one feel a little freer, suddenly you see the green skull, all these things that are so full of that punch he has. It hits you every time. That's not always the case with the artists they juxtapose him with. I saw Egon Schiele there once, he was an artist who was important to me when I was younger and had started drawing. But I never saw the originals until they came here, it took a long time, I was forty-five when I saw that exhibition. And they miss their mark. They're a little amateurish, Schiele died when he was twenty-eight, so what he comes up with is stuff you're already through with. It's very sexual, very physical and erotic, and very pubertal. Viewed against Munch it seems so *small*, so puny. It's nice, it's beautiful, but it stops there, and maybe that's what lets you accompany Munch the whole way, because he lived such a long life . . .

She held up the sheet with the exhibition pictures.

– This cabbage field, for instance, she said. – It works, though you can't really say why. It's just so simple. Technically it's so easy. He does it almost as an extension, what you see is what you get, and that's exactly what you want, since it speaks to you. All the time. It has that elegance. The best part about his pictures is precisely the simplicity, that he knows how to loosen it up. That there isn't this sense of being blocked. That it isn't stuck. Whereas what *is* stuck is what he's describing. Am I right?

– His best-known pictures are so charged, I said. – But then more and more he paints without that charge. What happens to quality then?

– Do you mean whether it's good *enough*, is that it?

– No, but what I'm thinking is, What is good? What makes a picture good? When the emotional charge is gone, what are you left with?

– Yes, I see what you mean, I've seen it many times in Munch's pictures. Since his production was so large, since there are so many pictures, it's easy to start looking for those that don't have that energy or that force, or those that are nothing much in themselves. When it's just a limp tree in purple and it doesn't really have what it takes.

– But what *does* it take?

– You know that when you're making something. It's not just this vague feeling, you yourself *know* when what you're making is good. It's like something has been solved. The pictures have it in them, they're a kind of total extension of oneself.

– Does a kind of freedom enter into it too? When it's just something being painted, and there is less and less ambition, when painting is almost all that's left?

– I struggle with that myself, I'm always trying to drain what I do of content. It's very demanding to be constantly stuffing so much into it, and the punch is there anyway if it's well articulated. Emptying the picture of content is often a very good idea. Not to be so strained. And often it's much more successful, I see that afterwards. Emptying it out. But I can't do it, I worry that it won't be enough. So I kind of screw my head into my arsehole. But when the pictures are good anyway, even though they've been emptied out, it's because they have it in them. They are an extension of what's in the body.

– Have you read Stian Grøgaard? Do you know him? I said.

– I don't like him.

– Right, I see. So you're antagonists, then. But I've talked with him, he had a lot to say about Munch, and he also looked through these late pictures. We talked about the ways in which these paintings are good and bad, and he pointed out the weaknesses of several of the ones I had chosen.

– That's always a useful exercise, walking around and finding the faults. I've done that many times.

– Yes, but to me, since I'm not a painter, it's interesting to hear how the pictures are judged from that point of view, how quality is viewed from there, from the other side. But actually I don't know what is good when it comes literature either, even though I write myself. Especially what I write myself. I like long descriptions of something which almost isn't there, long empty descriptions, if you can imagine such a thing, but I never know if one's any good, or how good it is – compared to a more psychological narrative with close-packed scenes, for instance.

– There's almost nothing there?

– Yes.

– But it's good anyway?

– In a way.

– Yes, and Munch has this ability, to put it up there and make it work, since the articulation is so good. Nothing is more difficult than that. It's not like pictures *contain* anything beyond what you see. It's actually very simple. Only a very few can manage that. Only a very few have it in them.

– Have what in them?

– A flow.

– A flow?

– Yes, a flow to get it all the way out. Even living a stationary or staccato life it can happen. It's like Tarjei Vesaas, who writes well sitting on a rock, without moving. And then it hits you anyway because it's a good way of seeing it, and then it doesn't matter so much what comes out on the other side.

There was a silence, we looked at the pictures among the glasses and plates on the table in front of us.

– I find that many of Munch's drawings can be quite trying. The way he sets them up, so graphically, can be annoying. They're so romantic. And they look constructed, and they don't harmonise musically.

She shook her head as she leafed through the folder.

– No . . . she said. – No . . . No . . . Many of the large pictures are tiring too, for there he has to *solve* it. And then you see the solution instead. It's fine, of course, I'm not saying it isn't, Jeez . . . that sun is quite nice. No . . . No . . . That one?

What's that? A naked man in the forest? That's a very weird picture. And something about it doesn't work. But the pink trunks are good.

– What do you think of that one? I said, nodding towards *Girls Watering Flowers.*

– Good God, no! It's embarrassing, really. But *this* one is very good. It's lovely, it's fantastic. *Three Men*, 1927. There he's really going for the jugular, right. He's out there raising hell. And this is a magnificent cabbage field. No one does cabbage like he does, as my mother says.

– So what do you think Munch himself was after, then, walking around at Ekely painting these pictures?

– Filling his life with something. What else was he supposed to do? I mean, I do it myself. It takes three days to get into it, if I have to travel somewhere and do something else, but I know what I need to do, I've been practising for so long. You just have to endure it. And then at first it's dead, right? Not necessarily bad, but it seems affected. Before it sort of starts to flow and you become a part of it yourself. And that's the only good place to be, really. Art isn't a therapeutic project, at least not to me it isn't. It's a way for me to get away from being therapeutic, and be free, do something else. It's a separate place. It's nothing other than that. So I don't find it strange that an old person like him did that. What else was he supposed to do? It's a way of being in the world which makes it possible. It can get very empty without it.

– And he cleared a space for himself so he could do it, didn't he, he didn't have any children . . .

– When I was studying at the art academy people were always telling me it was stupid to have children. There was a lot of talk about not having children, that it would get in your way. I totally disagreed. As if you could get in the way of yourself. But there is a conspicuous absence of children in contemporary art. How do you tackle it? When you have children yourself? They have to be there, right? When I had my first child, I made an exhibition with children, because it was such a huge part of my life at the time. It was troublesome to begin with, and then it became easier after a while. She was so lovely, you see, I just had to look and look at her. She would lie there next to my table, and on the table and under the table, and then it ended up as a huge exhibition. That children should stand in the way of an artist is a strange attitude. As if you're not supposed to be in touch with certain parts of yourself. And it's maybe that kind of idea people had about Munch, that he was this totally dedicated person. That we should somehow renounce, make sacrifices for him. But that's not what art is! You have to shove meaning into it and turn it into a possible place. Maybe not even meaning, after a while. Or maybe meaning. I don't know. I don't know what meaning is. That's always been a problem, telling a story. Because it gets seen as a literary project. It was a huge problem way into the 2000s. I went to the art academy when I was seventeen, and attended it for two and a half years. Then I got kicked out, and I moved to England and went to art school there. When I came back to Oslo in the 1980s, it was a problem for art to have content. What I think they meant by that was that you were supposed to get far away from yourself. The entire art world of Norway back then revolved around the relation to abstraction and form. They would talk about colour as if it had its own inherent value and stuff like that. The way they talked about art was abstract, the way they looked at art, and what you definitely shouldn't concern yourself with was recognisability. And what you did should absolutely not be a part of your self. So what do you do? That was one of the times I really struggled, one of the situations in which I didn't feel like painting.

– Why were you kicked out?

– Not because I wasn't working, it was rather that we disagreed about my project, what I was really trying to do. What I was doing had been unclear because I was a child, really. I was seventeen years old. Anger and frustration and all the things you go through, sex and terror and all that. But to return to a conversation after having been to England, where what I did was part of a tradition, where one had a language for it, where one talked about it, where one had writers come to visit – that would have been quite impossible here – and then to come back to this distanced and almost entirely abstract conversation, that was difficult. I mean, I understood what they were saying, but I disagreed with them about how something should be articulated visually. The rules were *very* strict. 'Literary' became a bad word, the moment a picture became literary, it became a problem. You could paint like Gerhard Richter, you could paint like the great important German painters, that was fantastic, but you couldn't bring anything personal into it, it couldn't be private, that was a big concern to them. It was almost a mantra. Or not almost, it *was* a mantra. Grøgaard was one of them. He was very particular about this. And there were many others like him. Professors who spoke of themselves as the way and the light. They were very preoccupied with Germany. But they didn't read. Well, maybe they read Hegel and stuff like that, they did, they related to what lay behind, in there in the darkness, as if it was another place. But it had nothing to do with the physical life. It was an impossible conversation, that wasn't what I was there for, I thought art was supposed to be an extension.

– Did you feel as if you were the problem?

– Oh yes. Definitely. But I still had my project that I kept going, I had had it since I was a child. Always, really. It was a separate place, in a way. But it was complicated because there was no room for it. The whole time I had to keep that inner pressure down, right, get rid of it. How do you do that? Abstraction doesn't come naturally to me, I don't recognise any of it, there was no purpose to it. Things just poured out of me. It was awful. The terror. Those were ugly years. And then Per Inge Bjørlo came along, he saved us. And Lars Vilks. He's an incredible guy. Extremely caring. He came in like some kind of prince and saved us. The ugly prince.

– What did he do?

– Talk with us. We talked.

– So who were the artists who met these criteria, then? Who were considered good at the time?

– Oh, I guess the best was maybe Bård Breivik. Tom Sandberg was more of a weirdo. A. K. Dolven. They filled out the whole field, and actually that was a relief, since I was never ready. I never wanted to make my debut, I was always anxious it wouldn't be enough. The first exhibition I had filled all of Bergen to the brim. That was in the Bergen Kunsthall. Not a single thing was written about it. This great big debut, and then there was nothing but silence. Dead quiet. Two hundred and twenty-eight pictures. I mean, huge ones. I wallpapered all of Bergen. But no one saw them.

*

As I left Vanessa and Kari and walked from the restaurant over to the hotel, all I thought about was that Vanessa Baird had been so critical of so many of the pictures I had selected for the exhibition. That she had used words like bad, feeble, shameful, embarrassing about them, and often laughed too, in a way I felt to be contemptuous. Next morning I was so full of shame and anxiety about the pictures that I could hardly get out of bed. As a writer, in the actual moment of writing, an absolutely necessary precondition is to be able to disregard what other people might think, and to be entirely alone with yourself, your thoughts and what eventually manifests itself on the page. For it isn't just the notions that you yourself have which exist before you begin to write – the equivalent of Deleuze's 'the painting before painting' – but also what others might think of those notions, that influences you too, and has to be fought. And yesterday and today, while I have been transcribing the recording of Baird, I have come to realise that that's what she was *really* talking about. The difference between the expectations that people around you have about what art is and should be, and the art you create. She brought what she had inside her to an art world that sought abstraction and considered art something fundamentally separate from the artist. She had children, she brought that experience with her into her art, and if it wasn't unheard of, it was still considered wrong. Her key word for art had been 'extension'. The conflict was similar to the one Munch had faced in 1885, almost exactly a hundred years before Baird began her art education, he too wanted to bring his own experiences into the art of his day, which in no way corresponded to what he had inside him. 'How can art be an extension?' – that might be one way to articulate the problem Munch had faced in his time.

How could I not have heard that as we sat talking in the restaurant before Christmas?

I had identified myself with the exhibition to such an extent, not with the pictures in themselves but with what they represented, that I was full of anxiety about how it would be judged. If the verdict was that it was weak, I would be humiliated, it would become obvious that I didn't know what I was doing, that they had handed over an entire museum to an idiot. If the verdict was that it was good, I could go on working on other things as if nothing had happened. To me, that was what the conversations with Grøgaard and Baird had been about, deep down. What I myself really thought about the pictures, or what I thought they were, no longer mattered, it was something blowing in the wind, drifting in the sea.

This was the opposite of integrity, the opposite of an act of art, for an act of art is precisely seeking something that can't be said or done in any other way, and which disregards the thoughts and opinions of others, is in fact entirely independent of them. Munch could not have painted *The Scream*, *Ashes* or for that matter *Elm Forest in Spring* if he hadn't disregarded what others might think of them. If he had paid any attention to the wind that was blowing, he would have painted *Morning* and variations of that until his death, like others of his generation in Norway. He had to take a risk, he had to dare the unknown, which entailed the danger that he would be ridiculed and humiliated. It sounds like a small risk to take, but it isn't, not if what we're talking about is your soul. That is why shame and doubt are a part of the artist's profession, but not of the work of art. That must be shameless and free of doubt. Doubt and shame are social mechanisms, they come into play when a boundary has been transgressed, when something is done or said that shouldn't have been. Art lives by transgressing boundaries, by going beyond what has been collectively decided, beyond what everyone has agreed to see and think. Shame is the sanction, but in order for it to be applied, there must first have been shamelessness. That the reactions to Munch's pictures were so strong initially, when a common reaction at the exhibition of *The Sick Child* was that people stood there laughing at it, was precisely because it had been painted shamelessly, with no thought of how it would be judged, entirely on its own terms. To Munch it was about a sister he had loved who had died when she was fifteen, and an attempt to keep that pain and those emotions open in the painting. Once one person had laughed, it was easy for the next person to laugh along, for if it isn't always comical when someone fails, it is when the distance between intention and result is so great – that is what they saw, a format and a motif which entailed something sublime and solemn, executed in a clumsy and amateurish way. They saw pretension, they saw someone who thought he was more than he was, and that's what they laughed at. Look, they said, the emperor has no clothes! That the emperor was in fact trying to arrive precisely at nakedness, they lacked the prerequisites to understand, how could they have known, such a picture had never been seen before. And laughing at failed pretensions on a grand scale is delicious.

The whole point of Munch's art when he made his breakthrough was that it was uncertain, there was no scale to measure it against – at least not in provincial Kristiania – there were no fixed criteria that could be employed to determine its quality. And that is when art is at its most interesting, when it is still uncanonised, still undecided. To judge it positively then demands as much integrity of the critic as creating it demanded of the artist. That is why almost the only people in Kristiania who didn't ridicule and humiliate Munch publicly were other artists and writers, like Krohg, Thaulow and Sigbjørn Obstfelder.

Now, in 2017, it's hardly a feat to point to Munch's greatness, there is no longer anything controversial about his pictures. That is why the exhibition with Bjarne Melgaard at the Munch Museum was so interesting. For even though Melgaard is an established artist in the global art world, his pictures are so ugly, childish, provocatively dumb, violent, aggressive and shameless that the question of their worth and quality becomes pressing when they are encountered alongside Munch's canonised pictures. Is this really art? Is this important? Isn't it just a provocation? It's just scribbling! How Melgaard will be judged fifty years from now is impossible to know. It is safest to say that he is a great artist, since his pictures are sold for dizzying amounts by leading New York galleries, and laugh at all those who don't understand it; but if you're being perfectly honest now, with yourself, is it really art?

But of course it isn't as simple as that, Melgaard isn't simply stepping into Munch's role as the artist against the bourgeois mob, for after the modernist breakthrough, which Munch was a part of, the unlearned, deformed, wild and unfinished have become expectations of art, so it's more that Melgaard sustains and affirms a certain language in that symbiosis with critics and gallerists which is formed by an art paradigm. It is difficult to imagine that a break as radical as that which took place in the 1880s and 90s will ever happen again – but then it was impossible for those living in the 1850s to predict that the old art paradigm was about to collapse.

My shame on account of a few pictures which perhaps wouldn't be considered good, and which I hadn't even made myself, merely selected, and the spineless fear which a couple of critical voices produced within me, can perhaps serve as an indicator of the power of social mechanisms, how they force everything into the channel of consensus, and what it must cost not just to oppose them, but to work within them – not as a curator, for that is nothing, really, nada, zero, nil – but as an artist, what forces are present even before one picks up the brush.

What Vanessa Baird was perhaps primarily doing when she spoke about Munch's pictures, was demythologising them, and thereby art in general. Art is important, but there is nothing great about it, there is no reason to elevate it, turn it into something that exists on a higher plane. The essential thing about Munch's art is that we recognise ourselves in it – that it is like us. And what we recognise is a little embarrassing, perhaps precisely because it is so common and cannot quite measure up to the church-like and sanctified position it has been assigned. Jealousy isn't an elevated emotion, it is a petty and silly and unworthy emotion. Melancholy, that touch of world-weariness, doesn't exist in isolation, but alongside the potatoes being peeled and the faint yellow light they fill the kitchen sink with when the peel has come off them, the cat in its winter fur looking like a rolling ball of wool as it dashes over the lawn, the voices on the radio talking about something perfectly unimportant in the background, the children suddenly shouting to each other somewhere in the house. And the breakdown which *The Scream* represents is just terrible, terrible.

– I don't hang out much with artists, Vanessa said. – Things get stuck that way, it becomes so important, everything becomes so hugely important. It's so interesting, they say. All of it is so very interesting. And then I think, go to hell, it isn't! It's a way of seeing things, a way of being, and you make certain choices, you shove a little meaning into the everyday, and the days go by. Because it gets dreary at times, right. It's not like you're having such a fucking great time always.

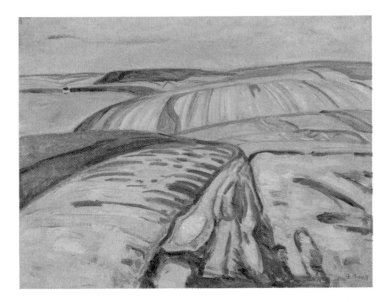

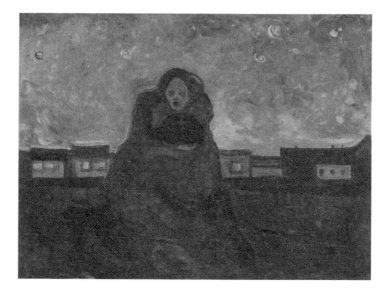

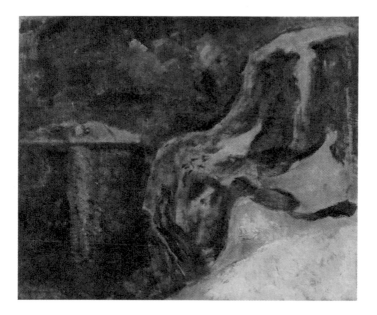

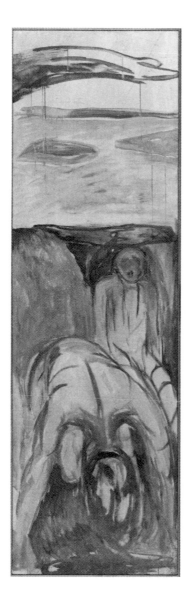

THREE

One of the best film openings I have seen is that of *Oslo, August 31st*, Joachim Trier's second feature film. It hardly gets any simpler: as we see living images of Oslo from the 1970s and 80s, some of them in the morning with deserted streets, others shot from a car driving through the city in the summer, glimpses of a public bath, glimpses of a park, glimpses of a beach, we hear a succession of different voices relating their memories of that same city. Every sentence begins with 'I remember'. They are private memories, of people we don't know, and yet we recognise them, we all have such memories. What this montage does is to weave together an enormous collectivity, for what you come to realise is that the whole city is full of people, all of whom are full of memories, criss-crossing time and space. That this opening moves me deeply every time I watch it isn't merely for nostalgic reasons – that the images show a city which no longer exists except in memory – but also because I feel such a powerful longing to belong to that collectivity, to that shared space.

That might sound odd, for I do belong to it, we all do, every single person in the world could relate their memories about a town or a place, and they would be interwoven with the memories of others. But that space is abstract, it is impossible to get to, it is made up of individual people who always find themselves in concrete situations, and it is these situations that we have to relate to, open up or remain on the outside of. The film that follows is about just that: instead of the city's all, we see the city's one, a gifted young man who meets various people in the course of one day, some who have meant a lot to him, others whom he encounters by chance. Common to all of them is that they wish him well, he is as it were enveloped in love, but he is unable to receive it, it runs off him, after a long day and a night he is exactly the same as at the beginning of the movie. He is a drug addict and has just spent time in a detox programme at an institution; the film ends with him injecting alone in an apartment early in the morning, and then we see in reverse order all the places he has visited in the past twenty-four hours, now deserted: what happened there is now merely a memory among all the others.

We learn almost nothing about his inner self, his thoughts or feelings, the important thing is the reactions he elicits from the people around him – similar to how Dostoevsky's *The Idiot* (1868) is more about the reactions to the protagonist than about the protagonist himself, who is unchanging, but in the opposite way, unchangingly open and loving – but during the film's final five-minute-long sequence it is as if we are given a glimpse inside him, as he sits down at a piano in the empty apartment and begins to play, just before he shoots himself up with heroin and passes out on the bed.

To narrate is already to compromise with truth, that is, with reality as it is, and that too has always been the role of art, to manipulate, to calculate, to measure out effect and cause, and nowhere is this manipulation greater than in film, which perhaps for this reason is not quite considered among the fine arts. It is much less free in relation to collective notions, that language about reality which we mistake for reality, what we, when it appears in its simplest form, call cliché, and which in an expanded sense falls within the rhetorical concept of *doxa*. Film is often affirmative, and perhaps that is its true role, that it builds a sense of community; after all we see it in a cinema together with others, and that is an important part of film's identity.

But it can also show us something which otherwise would not have been seen, or would not have been seen in that way, and it does so not through single images but through sequences, so it works with time, with what is changing, towards what is coming into being.

Precisely because film is a genre that addresses an audience so directly, and the theme of a film is so dependent on narration that it is almost always hollowed out by it, I have great respect for Joachim Trier; he succeeds in creating something that isn't hollowed out, he reaches in to something simple, human and powerfully emotional, from where significance begins to work its way outwards.

Oslo, August 31st begins in the collective, with memories we all have, while the rest of the film is about a rejection of community, of the others. We have no difficulty identifying with the protagonist, for we all know the conflict he embodies. This movie character sees through everything, everything that goes on around him is just empty talk, rubbish, banalities, and that's how it is, social life is just empty talk, rubbish, banality, and yet that's where we live our lives, and to turn one's back on it, or to be unable to take it in, can be fatal.

That the film shows this, with both perspectives effective throughout, both the people who give and he who doesn't want to receive, in my view makes it a significant work of art. And even though a hundred years separate it from Munch's *oeuvre*, and it not only plays out in another world but also represents an entirely different art form, and consequently there are no direct parallels, the fundamental thing in Munch's art is not the reduction of elements on the surface of the picture, the simplification of forms or a wild use of colour, but the conveying of what it means to be a human being in the world. By exploring his inner self, he explored everyone's inner self, the feelings he expressed were everyone's feelings. And one of Munch's main themes was the person who is shut up within himself, the person who shuts out the world – the man sitting with lowered head in *Ashes*, the man standing with lowered head in *Woman in Three Stages*, the man staring straight at us with the couple in love behind him in *Jealousy*. The woman sitting with lowered head in *The Sick Child*. The people in the sickrooms, each in their separate space, alone with themselves.

The distance between Oslo and Kristiania August 31st is great, but isn't it a fantastic thought that it is the man from *Ashes*, Munch's most mysterious painting, who gets up and walks away from the forest and into Oslo, where the life he encounters, which he shakes off, is our life, our conversations, our parties, our nocturnal baths, and that the apartment where he sits down to play the piano is our apartment.

That this could be so is because feelings never change, only our way of representing them. How to represent a

feeling in visual terms, how to represent a memory visually –
these are problems Joachim Trier engages with too.

*

I met Joachim Trier for the first time in New York, we were
supposed to take part in an event together to talk about place
and memory in film and literature, and met for breakfast in
the hotel restaurant on the same day. I didn't know much
about him except that he was a few years younger than me,
that he always gave good interviews, that he had once been
the Norwegian national skateboard champion, and that skat-
ing movies had been his way into film. He had a reputation
for being very nice and easy to get along with, perhaps a
rather unusual reputation to have in literary and artistic
circles.

We sat down in one of the booths and ordered coffee and
breakfast.

– I feel like telling you a secret, he said. – Something
hardly anyone else knows about.

And then he told me a story which made everything else
that was going on around us, all the comings and goings, the
small talk, the faces and laughter and clatter of cups and cut-
lery, disappear completely. There was a fire in him, and a
will to sincerity and self-searching which one simply couldn't
respond to with any kind of formality.

On stage that afternoon he was extremely articulate,
energetic and entertaining, while at the bar in the evening,
surrounded by his friends, he seemed carefree and light-
hearted, tuned in to them and what they shared.

During my work on the exhibition at the Munch Museum
plans for a film had also surfaced. At first I imagined that I

might visit Munch's various haunts, such as Åsgårdstrand, Kragerø and Ekely, perhaps also Berlin and Thüringen, primarily to write about them for this book, but of course I could also film a little with the camera on my mobile, capture the houses and the landscapes the way they looked now, talk a little about the pictures in a studio somewhere and edit it together with Munch's own film recordings and other material from that time, quite simply and unpretentiously.

When I got home from New York, it struck me that I could ask Joachim if he wanted to do it with me. He said he would like to, but he was working on a new film, they were in the pre-production phase now, they would be shooting it in autumn, and then he would be editing all winter and spring, so he didn't really have time. But, he said, his brother Emil directed documentaries, maybe he could do it, and then Joachim could join us on some of the days we were filming?

*

About half a year later Emil and Joachim picked me up at Oslo Central Station, we were going to Villa Stenersen at Vinderen.

In the car they told me that their grandmother had studied art history in Oslo in the 1940s, and that she and the other art history students had been given the task of cleaning up at Ekely when Munch died. So she was there, amid all paintings and the prints, in the chaos he had left behind.

– Have you ever talked to her about it? I asked them.

– We've tried, Emil said. – But she doesn't remember much any more. She's old now.

– Would have been great to include it in the film, though. An eyewitness account. She doesn't remember anything?

– Very little, I'm afraid.

According to Stenersen's biography, Munch passed away quietly at around six in the evening of 23 January 1944. He had caught bronchitis before Christmas, when he had spent several hours sitting thinly dressed in the stairway after some big explosions downtown. A German ship had been blown up, explosives had also been set off on the docks, a couple of hundred people died. All the way up at Ekely windowpanes shattered, and his housekeeper had made him take cover, where he caught the bronchitis which eventually weakened him so much that his heart stopped beating about a month later.

According to Sue Prideaux's biography, he was reading Dostoevsky's *The Possessed* in bed on the final afternoon of his life. The funeral was hijacked by quislings, although his sister Inger tried to prevent this; photographs of the occasion show a coffin covered with swastikaed wreaths. Munch himself had rejected every attempt by the Germans to make contact with him; Stenersen tells a remarkable story about the time when Knut Hamsun's son, the painter and writer Tore Hamsun, came to Ekely during the war to ask Munch to sit on an 'honorary board for the arts' together with his father, Christian Sinding and Gustav Vigeland. Stenersen gives the following account of the exchange between Tore Hamsun and Munch:

– You must accept membership on the board. My father is begging you – if, for no other reason, at least for the sake of old friendship.

– Old friendship? Is your father an old friend of mine?

– He speaks of you as the greatest painter of Scandinavia.

– Is that so? Does *he* have any of my pictures? That's news to me. Which ones does he have?

Tore Hamsun blushed. Knut Hamsun had no pictures.

– Perhaps he can't afford to buy any? Munch mocked.

The honorary board for the artists never materialised. Munch was unshakeable.[12]

It is difficult not to smile at this anecdote, especially if you know that Knut Hamsun was just as old, stubborn and wilful as Munch, and that they must have heaped curses on each other inwardly. Although they came from different social classes, Hamsun from the very bottom of society, Munch from the cultural elite, they had both had their breakthrough in the same city during the same time, with works that in similar ways represented a radical break with what had been, and both leaning on Dostoevsky. And both abandoned their early radical aesthetics and moved on to something else – Munch to a more traditionally observed painting, Hamsun to a more traditional narrative universe, both having absorbed vitalist impulses, the high point in Munch's case being *The Sun*, painted in 1911, and on Hamsun's part *Growth of the Soil* (1917). Munch's pictures of fields, horses and labouring peasants express a yearning to belong not all that dissimilar to that of Hamsun from that time. World War II was the great divide, Hamsun sided with the Germans, Munch kept his distance, and while Munch died in 1944, Hamsun lived on until 1952 and before he died wrote his masterpiece *On Overgrown Paths*, which is about the daily life of an aged man at an old people's home in Grimstad, where he has been interned pending the opening of his treason trial. The mood is not unlike that found in Munch's final self-portraits in his rooms at Ekely. The old man alone with himself and his mind.

To read about Munch and Hamsun is to read about something from a remote and long-gone era, but when Emil and Joachim told me about their grandmother, that she had been at Ekely that spring cleaning up, it struck me that it wasn't really that long ago. My parents were born the year Munch died, and the story my father told me, that he once saw Hamsun, might actually have been true, though it probably isn't.

The paintings, prints, drawings, letters and papers which the Trier brothers' grandmother helped to register are what now form the Munch Museum's collection.

*

Surrounded by old wooden houses and gardens, Villa Stenersen looks like something from the distant past, although it was built in the late 1930s. The villa, which was designed by the architect Arne Korsmo and represents a high point in Norwegian functionalism, shone in the rain as we came driving up the hill, with its facade divided into squares of blue- and white-painted concrete and grooved glass, veranda, staircases and columns.

There are photographs of Munch here, in one of them he is standing very erect in the living room, wearing an overcoat and with his hat in one hand and his cane in the other, it is slightly out of focus, so the details of his face are vague, but the way he holds his head, pulled back a little so that it looks like he is viewing everything from above, is recognisable from the portraits he painted of himself, including the very first ones, when he was a teenager in Kristiania in the 1880s.

In another photo Stenersen himself is there, he is standing right behind Munch and smiling broadly, looking astonishingly young compared to Munch, whose face is in sharper focus here: high forehead, slightly sunken eyes, thin white hair and an open mouth which makes him look very aged. That too is recognisable from the self-portraits, both the one where he is sitting and eating cod at a table at Ekely, the one where he stands looking grim in front of the window with the snow-covered landscape outside, and the one where he is standing very erect in his bedroom, between a clock with no hands and a bed.

When we reached the same living room and were standing in the same spot where Munch had stood in the photograph, so many time levels met. We were as distant from the 1940s as Munch had been from his own youth when he was here. In the photos taken at the villa then there is also a kind of break in time, the straight, sober and minimalist surfaces of the rooms made all the Munch paintings hanging there look old-fashioned, like something from another world or another culture. *The Dance of Life* hung there, and *Snow Landscape, Thüringen*, *Bathing Scene from Åsgårdstrand* and *Winter Night*, along with many others.

This was the second time I had stood in a room where Munch had been. The first was the one where he was born, in December 1863, and now this, which was one of the last rooms he visited.

Between the impoverished nineteenth-century room and

the extremely costly state-of-the-art modernist twentieth-century room lay his life and his paintings. And now another twist of the screw had been added, for the room was full of cameras, light and sound equipment belonging to the 2017 people making a film about him.

Joachim sat down in a chair in the middle of the floor, I sat in another, and one of the film crew snapped a clapperboard shut.

– Many of Munch's paintings from the 1890s are about being shut out, or about shutting the world out, I said. – It is almost as if he developed a symbolism of gestures of exclusion, with all the bowed heads and averted faces. That is clearly a theme in your films too. I am thinking among others of the main character in *Oslo, August 31st*, who is either unable or unwilling to receive anything from others.

– The first thing I want to say is that I feel a little embarrassed that you are asking me to compare myself with Munch. But let's talk about it as an inspiration. And as a part of the unconscious cultural field surrounding Munch. When I am making a film, I often don't understand quite what I'm doing until afterwards. What I realise then, is that the characters that interest me don't feel like outsiders initially – they are allowed to come to the party, they are allowed to be a part of the family, they are given the opportunity to form friendships, to belong to a city, to a milieu. But they are unable to get close to others. They don't know how to be among others. But they *are* among others. The Munch who is idealised in a lot of the biographical literature is the Munch who doesn't *want* to be among others. But in his pictures I see an enormous longing to be allowed among others. And that longing,

I have to admit when I look back at my films, it seems I have had myself.

– What is your relationship to Munch like?

– I began with the usual relationship to him that people who grow up in Norway develop. As a paradoxical figure whom we were told about, a master of sorts and an important national figure. At the same time, everything he stood for was very remote from what we faced in our daily lives, Norwegian values – for Norway isn't necessarily a country that cultivates art and intellectual pursuits – and all the things we love about Munch, his courage and his differentness, in everyday life were considered peculiar and excluded. But it took a long time before I was able to see his pictures. I felt about Munch the way some people feel about the Beatles: that the music is so iconised in the place you grow up that you just can't listen to it. You have to rediscover it. I did that with Munch via some of his woodcuts and lithographs, not through his paintings. I found the paintings too powerful, too garish. I thought it was all too much. I think I was afraid of his emotional honesty. In part it was also that when I was younger I was afraid of sentimentality.

– What was it that you were afraid of?

– I was primarily a film guy. Film is so mimetic, it is perhaps the most mimetic art form of all, and it is very easy to elicit emotion in a film. It's very easy to take the obvious and squeeze an emotion out of it. In literature there is a kind of automatic distance and abstraction, through the fact that it is writing. When you write yourself closer to reality, at the same time you are writing yourself closer to a separate literary space. In film you create a physical and *concrete* space. A person who suffers, the classic theme, a victim, you feel sorry for them – and then you squeeze the feeling for all it is worth. It's easy to do.

– Are you thinking of the manipulative side of it?

– Yes, the manipulation. That's why I always saw it through that particular optic. At the same time I had a genuine wish to be allowed to talk about intimate things that felt real and that no one talked about. I do think the reason we make art is because something is missing, there's a crack in the world, something or other isn't there, something has to be filled in – a meaning that isn't there. Which I am terrified will crush me. Maybe it sounds pretentious, but I think I've always been afraid of it. And then I look at Munch, who dares to speak in a personal and intimate idiom about the big things. Hegel talks about the universally specific. That you hit upon something so specific to you that it actually transcends you and reaches outwards. That's what I feel Munch does. The loneliness, the inability to get close to others, watching the others dance, standing in the forest and peering out at them on a summer night. I find it beautiful and deeply moving. And then there's the idea of mental spaces. That he actually creates a space I experience as being, almost concretely, a remembered space or a dreamed space. Which he dared to give form to. In an almost childish way, especially in the 1890s phase, the well-known stuff from the Frieze of Life, some of them are so *shameless* in their insistence that 'I'm trying to find an essence here'. To be faced with that has been a great inspiration for me.

– What is it about Munch's remembered spaces that interests you? Or memories in general; your films too are preoccupied with memory?

– Among my most powerful childhood experiences was

the realisation that we remember. I remember sitting on a tricycle when I was in kindergarten, and I thought of that moment and decided to remember it for the rest of my life. I still remember it. And I think that the moment you become conscious of your memories, you also become conscious of transitoriness and identity. When I was four or five years old I began to realise that time passes, because I was able to remember what I experienced. If time passes and I have changed, that means that I can also cease to be. I can get to the end of time. For human beings are not eternal. Then death appears. Instantly, like a connection: if I can exist, and remember that I exist, I can also not exist. I began to think about it a lot. And ever since then I have been preoccupied with my memories. I romanticise the past tremendously. Because the past is a place where I'm in control. I can't die there, because I survived. I was there, I remember it. And I know what the outcome was. I'm afraid of what is going to hit me, I'm afraid of what I don't know, I'm afraid of the future. I have difficulty being present, being in the moment. But I manage it retrospectively. And I sometimes manage when I'm making something. When I'm shooting a film, I know that what I'm making will also exist outside myself. That it takes time: film and memory are linked as formats. Melancholy is also about memory, and about transitoriness. It's mysterious to me, it is one of the things I care about most. Memories are identity, they are what we think of as ourselves.

– Transitoriness is really loss, and memory reconciles us to it. When someone dies, the issue of memory becomes acute in a whole new way. And uncertain. Your last film, *Louder Than Bombs*, plays out somewhere around there, in that territory. A mother kills herself, and you tell the stories of those who are left behind?

– I was interested in three men who were faced with the absence of the same woman. The husband feels wholly inadequate in relation to his children and to his wife, and he is unable to move on. When he meets another woman three years later, he can't handle it, he doesn't know what to do. The eldest son is unable to be a man in relation to his wife, he is unable to be a father to his child, and he is unable to acknowledge that maybe he didn't really know his mother. He distances himself from her after she dies. And then there is the youngest brother, who may have understood more but who hasn't been permitted to know, has been kept away by the others, but perhaps knows more than the others. As a child he is both more vulnerable and more malleable, he accepts time and experience in a different way. It is of course also about the things we idealise and then cannot move on from. Which is what happens when we lose someone. Very easily. The way Munch depicts the loss of both his mother and his sister Sophie is almost religious, almost erotic. You get a feeling of an incredible longing that is almost directly linked to the experience of new women, as transference. Which he then paints. His relation to woman as first an object of loss and then an object of desire, and the eternal rejection which he appears to stage in his paintings. In *Vampire*, is he being comforted or is he being killed? Is he being enclosed in something warm, or is he being removed from himself and life? Is she good, is she evil? Woman is an enormously complex entity in Munch's work. And one of the things I have been struck by in his pictures, perhaps because I am interested in it myself, is precisely that. Too near or too distant in relationships. And then I've been interested in the relationship between the traumatic and the sublime.

– What do you mean by that?

– If one considers the sublime as something which appears but can neither be articulated nor reduced, and the traumatic as that which becomes fixed within us, and which we can never remember clearly because it is too complicated. I thought of that in regard to Munch, how he keeps dwelling on those portraits of grief, those moments of sorrow, and of the enormous love for his sister as she somehow fades away. It is almost graphic in his paintings, she fades away into brushstrokes which no longer have direction, only a kind of diffuseness. And you can also see how *thoroughly* he has worked around some of the people he loved, erasing and painting over again, there is this texturing in the paintings which is so full of *nerve*. You feel the process. But trying to say it is a struggle. Trying to remember. Which in itself tells you that it was something traumatic.

– You spoke earlier about being afraid of sentimentality. I suppose it also has to do with wanting to make something that is true? Something that isn't manipulative or schematic. In *Louder Than Bombs* everyone in the family has particular roles, and everyone seems uncomfortable with them, they move in and out of them, not wholeheartedly, not as a result of a decision, it is more as if they are unable to do or be what is expected of them. They are between roles, in a way. That position reminds me of the act of making something, for then too one has a role, an expectation of how things should be. My thought is a simple one: that life really takes place between the forms, and that in order to get close to it, one has to get in between the forms that art has to offer. I am fairly certain that this was the problem Munch faced, not least when he painted his sister's death: how to find a way into what is real without using the effects and methods of realism.

– For me one of the most important things when I make a film is to try to find a language that fits formally with exactly what I want to do. To use the possibilities of the film idiom to create mental images. How can one show thoughts on the screen? A very concrete example: when we wrote *Louder Than Bombs*, we had a trite and simple formal idea – someone hears someone else reading from a novel, and that becomes thoughts. We knew that the boy was in love with a girl at school, and that we were going to tell the viewer that he didn't quite know what had happened to his mother. So we thought we could use that formal device, which is just cold and technical, and make it warm by putting it into play. We had written a literary pastiche, from something that might have been a novel, about someone who experiences the final moments of his life, and then we let the boy hear a girl reading it. He thinks about it, what the final moment of life is like, and then he wonders what his mother was thinking when she died, and the voice changes, he begins to think about how she died – was that how it happened? Maybe it happened like that, maybe not, he doesn't know. But he wonders. Did she think of him? Then he enters his mother's mind, and we cut in associations about what she may have been thinking of one time at the beach, for those are the kinds of moments we remember, with sand against our skin and wind – or did she think about me that time we were playing hide and seek? But wait, I was playing hide and seek there, she must have seen me the whole time! He discovers something about what his mother may have been thinking of him inside his memory, and before we know it, we are on the outside again, back in class. We have been on an internal journey, where I have tried, in a banal way, to create inner images, an inner stream of memories and thoughts. And in that stream an oedipal connection surfaces, which I didn't see at the time but understood later, between Melanie, whom he is in love with, and his dead mother. And it is true, in fact, that *is* what it's like to be a human being. But it's not something you can plan for, you have to stumble your way into it. *That* is exciting to me, using the film idiom to try to create montages like that. Many are opposed to it, they consider it unfilmic – they think film is about grand images giving form to situations. André Bazin, the great film theorist, says that one should be able to choose where to look, and that therein lies the humanism in film. One shouldn't force montage and manipulation upon the viewer. To me, that scepticism is comparable to being sceptical of sentimentality. Both result in a narrow space in which to feel and think. That form, which many film-makers call construed or strained or manipulative, is one I like to experiment with, and to me that's OK as long as you use it to get somewhere that is emotionally open.

– You talked about moments that can't be planned. Film involves a lot of planning, the script is written beforehand, and scenes are drawn. You also talked about the sublime. To me, that is something that can't be produced at will or calculated. How do you relate to that concept in regard to film?

– That's a good question, and it is a big question. What is the sublime? I think of the sublime in the classical sense, not just as a quality but as something in which elements of form and content go beyond the expected, become greater than themselves. That something transcends. Film has a lot to do with presence, the there-and-then-ness of something, where thoughts and abstractions are concrete, you can see them, they are clear and transparent, but you can't always grasp them. A sublime moment is a moment which has found a unique form, a unique expression.

– Can you think of an example?

– There is a very well-known scene in Tarkovsky, in *Mirror* (1975). It is a childhood memory, we are in a small wooden cottage, the first image is almost like a tableau and feels like a memory that could have contained all of time. It is empty, and when I look at it with the eyes of a director, I think: this place has been lived in. Someone has been a child here, someone has been old here, someone has died here. It is as if we are viewing something outside time. Suddenly the camera starts to move, without cuts – the whole scene is shot in one take – and we see some children running through the room, but we see them in a mirror, and when it's empty, we hear them from the outside, they are shouting that there's a fire. And then we see that the cowshed is in flames. At the same time it's raining. And there is nothing anyone can do. It is there and then, it is happening now, in this moment and in the same time-image, for there are no cuts – time flows at twenty-four frames per second – and yet we have moved from the eternal room to the momentary. We realise that this is a moment they will never forget. It is as if the world falls apart. Water co-exists with fire, which those two elements are not supposed to do. And no one can do anything. The world functions on its own, and that is a great insight, both for the children and for their mother. They are just standing there waiting, no one is panicking, they are simply observing this momentous event as it unfolds.

I had to see the film many times before I began to understand why it moved me so powerfully. There are so many time levels in that scene, so many states, which it really shouldn't be possible to combine. And then it is uniquely filmic. It couldn't have come about in any other art form than film.

*

Some months later I met Joachim and Emil again, they picked me up outside the Grand Hotel in Oslo early one morning, we were going to Åsgårdstrand to film Munch's house there and the landscape in which so many of his pictures are set. *Melancholy*, the troubled male figure sitting by the water's edge with the sky undulating above him; *Summer Night's Dream (The Voice)*, the woman who stands beckoning and looking straight at the viewer from the forest, with the shoreline and the sea visible between the tree trunks; *Girls on the Bridge*, the girls leaning against the railing of a jetty with a luminous house and a big dark tree in the distance – all of them show a recognisable, identifiable piece of reality, and it is found in Åsgårdstrand.

Except for a school trip to Knut Hamsun's home at Nørholm when I was fourteen, I had never before sought out places from the world of art or literature; the pilgrimage aspect of it was alien to me, indeed it seemed almost obscene. All around Stockholm there are plaques with quotes from poems and novels that are set in the place where the plaques are placed, and when I lived there I found them nauseating, it seemed so wrong, for even though the text describing

Västerbron in Eyvind Johnson's *Krilon* is about Västerbron, or the text describing Tegnérlunden in Astrid Lindgren's *Mio, My Son* is about Tegnérlunden, those two entities, the fictitious one – no matter how realistically it was described – and reality itself, had nothing to do with each other. They existed in two different and sharply separate spheres, which shouldn't and really couldn't be brought together.

This wasn't anything I could present a reasoned argument for, it was just a feeling I had, and I wondered how things would turn out in Åsgårdstrand, where the artistic point of departure wasn't literary but visual.

That both the Grand Hotel and Karl Johan Street were motifs Munch had painted and that both the hotel facade and the layout of streets from that time were intact did not cross my mind. Nor did I think about the fact that Munch and his artist friends used to sit drinking at the Grand, that Ibsen was a regular, or that it was on Karl Johan Street that the young Munch saw his first great love, Milly Thaulow, promenading with her husband and children, or for that matter that this was where the nameless protagonist of Hamsun's *Hunger* would lope about. I had my own memories of Oslo, they shone with a stronger light than whatever my memory had stored of events and people I had read about, and that's how it must have been for those who had been there back then too, Edvard Munch, Hans Jæger, Oda Krohg, Christian Krohg, Sigbjørn Obstfelder, Aase Nørregaard, Milly Thaulow, Knut Hamsun, they too must have felt that history and the past dissolved in the present, and that the present was fluid, improvised, accidental, never entirely unknown but still never quite established – Hamsun wasn't 'Hamsun', just Hamsun, perhaps even just Knut, a self-assured, pugnacious and wilful young man with a hard carapace who wrote news-paper articles about all kinds of things, and Munch wasn't 'Munch', just Munch, perhaps even just Edvard, a sensitive, self-absorbed, often sarcastic young man struggling to free himself of his bonds to home and family without quite suc-ceeding. Both had dreams of greatness, but neither knew if they had it in them, or what it really was. Knut wrote, Edvard painted. How many young people with similar ambitions are there in the world? That both of them did have it in them – not greatness, but actually its opposite, a smallness great enough, or sufficient will to explore smallness, Hamsun with his petty street fights and scenes in public, Munch with his personal memories and feelings of inferiority – the people around them may or may not have understood, either way it would have been in a very different way than we under-stand it, since 'Munch' and 'Hamsun' to us are known entities, a kind of emblem, something they obviously never were to themselves, nor to the people around them, not even towards the end of their lives, when they were Norway's great-est artist and greatest writer respectively. The cult which has arisen around their names, the whole field of associations which they evoke, are like a screen between us and their works, and between them and their lives. Biographers always write to get beneath the myth and the notions clustering around their names, they try to pierce through to the life and the time as it really was, which often gives rise to a new imbalance – I have read biographies about Munch, about Hamsun, about Ernest Hemingway, about Aksel Sandem-ose, about Agnar Mykle and about Jens Bjørneboe, all of them have powerful myths attached to their names, and all have been portrayed as curiously petty people, in the sense that they were full of serious failings, weaknesses, foolishness and unpleasant personality disorders. Afterwards it was impossible to understand how that person could have written that book or painted that picture. Bjørneboe was perhaps the worst. After reading his biography I got out the books in his trilogy *The History of Bestiality* (1966–73). I needed only to read a few sentences to see that the man about whose life I had just read, *couldn't* have written this. It was impossible for a man like 'Bjørneboe', as he was depicted, to have written something so sensitive, insightful and wise, with such presence in the writing. The same applied to Mykle and Hemingway, and to an even greater degree to Sandemose and Hamsun. Why is that? I think that writing about another human being, regardless of how objective one struggles to be, can only be done within the framework of the person writing, in other words the biographer. And since a life is always full of weaknesses, foolishness, triviality, quirks, mistakes, pride and cowardice, indulgence and ambition, the biographer, since he or she sees this, will always stand above their subject, it is almost inevitable. But a person is not a person merely from the outside, is not merely the sum of encounters with others, a person is first and foremost a person to themselves, and that is the place one writes from, that is the place one paints from.

After reading Bjørneboe's biography it is easy to think that he was rather stupid. When you read a book by Bjørneboe you realise that he was anything but stupid. The same is true of Munch. It may sound a little strange, but I have always underestimated Munch, in my eyes he seemed a bit dumb, a bit naive, someone who didn't understand very much, neither of himself nor of other people. That he was able to paint so well in spite of this, I have thought of more or less as a matter of luck, or that painting is so different from thinking that even a rather stupid fellow might hit upon something. This image of Munch has rarely reached my consciousness in the form of articulated thoughts, it has been more of a vague feeling I have had about him. It wasn't until I read Sue Prideaux's biography about him, *Behind the Scream*, that I caught sight of my prejudice. There he is portrayed at eye level, he isn't a person the biographer looks down on, and he emerges as a real person, rather like you and me, an existentially searching and very intelligent man, with an experience of loss that marked him and deepened his insight into life. I don't mean to say that he was a genius, I don't know what genius is, and I suppose I don't really believe that such a thing exists among people, only that the insight found in his pictures wasn't accidental, and that it didn't have anything to do with his ability to draw, although the ability allowed it to be expressed. The iconic 'Munch' can easily take the life out of his pictures, the biographical 'Munch' can easily take the pictures away from the life.

*

It was cold on the morning we were going to Åsgårdstrand, minus five degrees, and the still pitch-black sky was covered with fog. People on their way to work walked by as I stood waiting outside the Grand Hotel, the sound of their footsteps ricocheting between the facades of the buildings, and I remembered how Oslo could be, that peculiar silence in the streets, how people walked by without a word, and how that feeling of silence could be there even when groups of people talking went by, dissolving their footsteps and words.

A black car came driving down the pedestrian street and pulled up on the pavement. It was Emil and Joachim. I climbed in, into the warm, faintly humming interior, and we drove out of Oslo, along roads and past buildings I wouldn't have noticed fifteen years earlier but which I now saw and thought of as being Norwegian. All the spruces, the hills and hillsides, all the wooden houses, the yellow road signs and the yellow dividing line, the small boat marina. The bus sheds made of concrete embedded with pebbles. The small Norwegian flags on the number plates, Emil and Joachim's manner and jargon, so different from the Swedish I was usually surrounded by.

Our own culture envelops us, and at times it can feel suffocating because so much of it affirms us, but when you have been away from it for a while, this enveloping feels good, the affirmation it offers feels almost healing.

That's what I was thinking about as we drove south while dawn rose, with the fog suspended between the trees and over the fields which suddenly opened up in places. And then I thought how strange life was, which had now led me here, to this very car with these very people, to walk in the footsteps of a man who had been dead for more than seventy years, and whom I had learned about in school a long time ago.

After less than an hour we left the main road and turned off towards Åsgårdstrand. The fog was so dense that I couldn't get an overview of the town, all one could see were the streets we drove on; in the direction where I assumed the fjord must lie there was just a wall of grey.

The other members of the film crew were standing in a car park, waiting outside in the cold. We parked next to them, and Joachim and I each got a microphone clipped to our jackets before we headed down the road with the camera first in front and later behind us. The streets looked roughly the way they must have looked a hundred years ago, with their old white wooden houses and little gardens. When I turned round and looked up the road, I recognised one of Munch's motifs, a street with some children lying on the roadway and a girl peering out of the picture. That must be from here, I thought. It gave me a strange feeling, for some things were recognisable while others were not, and the recognisable part was so intangible that it reminded me of a dream that springs to mind and which slips further and further away the more you try to remember it.

There wasn't a soul in sight, no activity anywhere, only the motionless houses and the empty street.

Within one garden there was a rock formation, twisted and volcanic-looking, like frozen lava except that the rocks were greyish.

– He painted those rocks, I said. – One of the pictures in the exhibition must be of them, I'm almost sure of it.

– Shall we have a look? Joachim said.

Standing in front of the rocks I became uncertain, for the picture I was thinking of looked almost like stones on a heath with the ocean in the background, while here they lay in the middle of a housing development. At the same time there was no mistaking the shape of the rocks, it had to be them.

Since then I have seen those rocks in many of his pictures from Åsgårdstrand and realised that he never went very far away to paint – the rocks lay perhaps fifty metres from his house, and most of his town pictures were painted in that same stub of a road. Many of the beach pictures are from the beach just below the house, and many of the garden pictures from his own garden. It wasn't just local, it was extremely local.

I liked it so much, seeing how small and narrow the world of his motifs was. Those rocks could have been something one remembered from childhood, rocks one used to play on, or they could have been something one barely registered on one's way to the shop to buy bread rolls in the morning. In the pictures they had a very particular significance, as a place in the world, by the sea, beneath the sky, there they were existentially charged, painted as a painter would have painted Calvary or another place of great importance. But in itself Calvary is just a hill like any other, its importance has been assigned to it by us. By giving the same attention and weight to all his motifs, Munch demonstrated that to be a human being in the world is the same everywhere, and that significance lies within ourselves. Therefore, laundry hanging from a clothes line in the garden can have as much existential weight as a biblical or mythological motif. Or some peculiar-looking rocks in a garden in a small Norwegian seaside resort.

We walked on, still with the camera crew in front of us.

– That must be his house, Joachim said and nodded towards a small ochre house on the other side of the road. And sure enough, on the wall hung a white sign with the words MUNCH'S HOUSE.

– It's so small! I said.

– Almost like a cottage, Joachim said. – Shall we go down into the garden and have a look?

The garden behind the house was narrow but long, descending rather steeply towards a beach.

– The picture of the fight with Ludvig Karsten must have been painted around here, he said. – Karsten is lying here, and Munch is standing here, and then the house is back there.

– You're right, I said. – But the house seems so much bigger in the painting!

We walked up to the front of the house again, where a woman stood waiting for us. She told us that everything inside was the way it had been when Munch died, except that it wasn't as messy as it had been then. We bent our heads and went in. The white winter light fell softly into the room, which was strikingly small: a writing desk beneath the window, a bed by the wall, a cupboard in the corner. A small kitchen within, and then a small bedroom with another bed, that was all. We walked around in there for a while, looking at things; his winter coat hung on a peg, on another hung a suit jacket and a waistcoat, in the corner cupboard stood bottles of medicines, turpentine, tubes of paint and a well-worn palette. Below stood a pair of black dress shoes, they were small, size 42 at most.

– Well, well, I said. – So this is where he lived.

– He had his studio down there, the woman said. – It was torn down, but it's been rebuilt to look the same as it was.

I tried to picture him, lying on the bed, standing in front of the window, sitting and drinking with his friends in the next room, one of those liquid evenings that there must have been so many of. The quarrel with Tulla Larsen which ended with him waving a pistol about and accidentally shooting himself in the finger.

But all I could see was the room here and now, so museum-like and looking rather contrived, since the authenticity wasn't a result of life being lived here but rather of time standing still. The film crew walking around filming, Joachim standing there and looking around.

– I'm not really much in favour of a biographical approach to art, he said.

– Me neither, I said.

– But here we are.

– In Munch's house. And I've touched Munch's overcoat!

– I think the beach from *Melancholy* is down there, Emil said. – Though there's some contention about it, it might also be from a beach a little further down.

– Well, let's go down there, then, Joachim said. – And see if we can find the *Melancholy* beach.

A few minutes later we were standing on the beach, next to a boulder that was larger than the others, discussing whether or not this was the *Melancholy* rock.

– If it had been here, there should have been forest there, Joachim said, pointing inland. – As far as I remember?

– But that pier out there seems right, I said. – And the line of the beach fits. They could have cut down the forest since then, no?

– Well, sit down then, let's see!

I sat down on the rock, supported my chin on my hand. I couldn't keep from smiling.

– That's not melancholy! Joachim said.

– I know, I said. – But it isn't easy to be melancholy with so many people watching. Try it yourself!

Joachim sat down, chin in hand, a doleful look on his face. The beach curved away behind him, ending at the jutting pier, but it was much shorter, entirely lacking the depth of the painting.

– It isn't here, I said. – Let's try the next one!

We approached the next cove from the forest, and I recognised the beach and the sea between the tree trunks: it was from here that so many of his pictures had been seen. And when we got down to the beach, we saw that its curving edge resembled the shoreline in *Melancholy*.

It felt very peculiar. The experience was rather like the feeling one sometimes gets visiting a childhood haunt, how shockingly small everything seems. I thought about a time a few years ago when I drove to my grandparents' house in western Norway together with my own children. The roads were much narrower than I remembered, the distance was shorter, and the place that in my memories was one of the centres of the world in reality lay on its very periphery. And then the two main rooms in the house, which in my recollection were vast halls, full of objects and things happening, but in reality were tiny and rather wretched.

It wasn't just that this forest was so small, whereas in the paintings it was The Forest, and that the beach was so commonplace, while in the paintings it was practically mythological, it was also that the forest and the beach were so shockingly concrete, and seemed to reject the images in my mind.

The present is so powerful because it is the only thing that exists, all the rest is simply notions we have, which in themselves have neither form nor shape nor weight. When I stood in my grandparents' rooms, the present with one blow knocked down all memories, although there were hundreds of them, spanning more than twenty years.

And yet it would be a big misunderstanding to think that whatever has no form, no shape and no weight – in other words, our thoughts, feelings, notions, ideas, memories, mental images – always dissolves in the presence of the reality of the now. One could also argue the opposite, that reality is something we have learned how to see, that it appears in and affirms an image we have beforehand. Of course, it isn't that simple either, but the fluid zone between the world in itself and our image of it is what painting explores, that is its core activity. That we still remember Munch, and that his art is still alive in our culture, is because he went further in exploring that territory than most of his contemporaries.

But in what way is his art still alive? The actual pictures exist in actual places – most of them in museums – in the same way that the motifs they depict exist in concrete places. But it isn't in the realm of the concrete that they live on, it is in our notional world, in the minds of each and every one of us.

*

Some weeks before Christmas I saw that a picture by Munch had been put up for sale on a Swedish auction site I sometimes visit, it was a portrait of a woman from 1904, one of the many thousands of prints he had made in the course of his long life. It had never struck me before that one could actually buy a picture by Munch. A painted version of *The Scream* had been sold in 2012, it went for more than 120 million dollars. But there were so many of the prints, and they weren't original in the same way as the paintings, so they were within financial reach, this one cost roughly the same as a six- or seven-year-old Volkswagen Golf.

I enlarged the image on the screen. The portrait was very

simple, it seemed almost to have been drawn with a single line, and it was beautiful. I thought, damn it, I'll place a bid. Then I thought, come on, Munch on the wall, what kind of people have that? Old men and women belonging to the bourgeoisie, rich people who have either inherited the picture or bought it as a status symbol. But what kind of status did it give? Nothing I wanted to identify myself with, in any case.

In many ways I experienced the world in the same way I did when I was twenty, it was as if identity changed much more slowly than life, it crept forward like an oil tanker, and I was the tanker, while the small speedboats and cabin cruisers which surrounded it on all sides were the events it related to. When I was twenty, bourgeois life was the worst thing imaginable, it had to be transgressed in every conceivable way. The ideal, which was never articulated, not even vaguely thought out, lay fairly close to the life of a band on tour, or how I imagined this to be. Long nights of drinking, music and a steady stream of girls, the hedonism balanced by a radical, alternative and burning political conviction. This was childish, but as I said, it was a twenty-year-old's idea of life. And it was still with me, usually repressed, in the sense that I never thought through where I had ended up in life, what I did and why, what kind of values this expressed, but sometimes, perhaps if I read an interview with a band or came across a novel where that kind of existence was described, I might feel a wild and untamed urge to drink and go to ruin, just travel to some city, Stockholm, Copenhagen, Berlin, London, and go on a drinking spree. Write a little, perhaps, but mainly just live. Take the ferry to Poland and drive down through Europe, stay in cheap hotels in ever-changing towns, drink, drink, drink.

The odd thing was that I felt like that, like someone who

really lives that way, even though absolutely everything in my life represented the very opposite. I had a property with three houses on it and a garden I loved to be in and tend, and I had also bought the neighbouring house and the garden belonging to it, so that most of my spare time during the summer half of the year was spent keeping it all in order. I had four children and tried to raise them properly, I didn't tolerate swearing and put my foot down on slovenliness or disorder whenever it appeared. The house was full of toys and school things, stuffed animals and iPads, and when I drove the children to and from school, it was with the sound of their horrid commercial pop hits streaming from the speakers. I made it a point of honour to keep the house tidy, and to make sure the children went to school properly dressed, did their homework and behaved politely to grown-ups. That I failed on all scores is a different matter. But apparently none of this left any trace on my identity, there I was still a twenty-something-year-old man who wanted to be a writer, and who only accepted what in one way or other could be considered alternative in life.

There was no way I could hang a picture of Munch on my wall.

But oh, how beautiful it was.

And it was alive, after more than a hundred years her gaze was still alive.

Buying this picture, wasn't that actually a way of not giving a damn?

Yes, it was. That would make me someone who didn't give a damn about anything.

It felt good.

*

Two days later, ten minutes before the auction closed, I placed a bid. Only one other bid had been registered, and it was low. Sometimes you could pull off a coup on this kind of site, I knew that, occasionally fantastic pictures go almost unnoticed there, so that you can get them at even less than the asking price.

A few minutes passed, then I was outbid.

So some bastard was out there who also wanted the picture.

I placed a new bid.

It might just be that the other bidder didn't want the picture as strongly as I did, and that my new bid, arriving so quickly that it signalled ruthlessness, or so I felt, would frighten him or her away.

But no. A counter-bid ticked in immediately.

I waited a little while to give the bastard hope, let him or her sit there and fill up with joy at having succeeded, at having acquired the picture, and then, when there were only a few minutes left, I placed a new bid.

Ha!

After only a few seconds the bastard raised his bid. At the same time the deadline was extended. The price of the picture was already higher than I had decided beforehand that I was willing to pay, but this was no longer about money, it was about winning, crushing the other bidder, whoever it might be.

And finally, after a new round, it went quiet.

The picture was mine.

Over the next few days I thought occasionally of all the other things I could have spent the money on. A fantastic holiday which the children would remember for the rest of their lives. Or redecorating the house, the children were big now, but not all of them had their own room yet, they would soon need one. Instead they got a little picture on the wall. A fruit press so that we could make juice from the apples and pears in the autumn, I had been thinking of that for a long time but hadn't bought one since the expense seemed unnecessary, it was too much money for something that would only be used once a year. And besides, it would make us even more bourgeois.

At the same time I visited the website and looked at the picture several times a day. I had worked on Munch's pictures for a whole year, leafed through the volumes with his paintings countless times, and was also familiar with the book containing his collected graphic works. Many people, especially artists, considered Munch a greater graphic artist than painter, that his greatest talent lay there. He could capture a motif with few means, while also intensifying it, often almost brutally, or coarsely. This picture wasn't like that, on the contrary it was delicate, a woman's head drawn with a few lines, her gaze and thereby her presence remarkably alive.

It didn't say who she was, so it was probably a model. The title was *Head of a Woman*. It was dated 1904, by then Munch was already moving away from Symbolism and entering the long phase during which he lived within his art, and his pictures were like one long story about the place where he had taken refuge, and in all imaginable forms from brief notes and messages to epic works.

This is to mythologise him, the solitary artist. And few artists in Norway have been more mythologised than Munch. He did it himself while he was alive, tying together his work and his life through suffering, and that notion still stands even though every single art historian who writes about him emphasises again and again that this is a myth, that he wasn't solitary at all but was in touch with people all over Europe, and that he was an entrepreneur in relation to his own career, which he painstakingly and intelligently built and managed, and that it wasn't his genius that found expression in paintings like *The Scream* or *Vampire*, but rather the spirit of the time, and that he was just one of many who gave expression to it.

All of which is true of course.

There is something about painters that causes myths or notions to spring up about them easily, perhaps because what they create is without language, the spaces they produce are without concepts, and these spaces, always enigmatic, must be explained. Since the 1960s most tendencies within the humanities have been towards the non-individual and de-centred, from structuralism, which was exclusively concerned with a work's internal coherence, to post-structuralism and postmodernism, feminism and postcolonialism, but despite more than fifty years of theorising about the aesthetic, social and political contexts of art, the Great Artist is still a dominant figure in the public sphere, both historically, through the continual recycling of the divinities of modernism and pre-modernism, such as Manet, Monet, Cézanne, Picasso and Pollock, and for that matter Munch, exhibited in ever new contexts and combinations at the great museums, and now, with the epithet 'the world's greatest living artist' alternating between Hockney, Kiefer, Richter and a handful of others.

This is so not only because our reality has been so commercialised, I think; the urge to canonise seems almost inherent to the human condition, as a way of assembling valuables, creating places where they become visible. Homer is one such place, Aristotle and Praxiteles are such places, and of course it isn't true only of men, Virginia Woolf, Hannah Arendt and Simone de Beauvoir are other such places, where something important is concentrated and becomes visible and possible to relate to. All artists wish to be raised to that level – those who deny it are either lying to themselves or to us – but if one gets there, as Munch did, only one side changes, the side facing outwards, towards others, while the side facing inwards, towards art, remains the same. Perhaps the painting before painting has grown, in the sense that there are more prior notions about what something is or should be, and especially about what has worked before, that have to be combated, but the practice itself is unchanged: the canvas, the brush, the colours.

What is admirable about the late Munch is that he succeeded in breaking down all notions of his own greatness as he worked, and that he managed to break with the formulas he had been successful with previously, so that in every picture he began anew, from scratch: this tree, this forest, these colours. One of the last pictures he painted was *Painter by the Wall*, it dates from 1942 and depicts a man standing on a ladder painting the wall of a house. It has nothing to do with Munch's inner life, it is a scene of everyday life that just happens to occur where he is, and which he paints. He doesn't even paint it particularly well, but quickly and carelessly. The painter's body is hardly more than a couple of brushstrokes, and the background just a little hastily raked-up green signifying grass and shrubs and some yellow and red-brown shapes indicating flowers. In the background there is a red barn, it lends depth to the picture and draws the viewer in, in the simplest way imaginable.

We can't get much further from the distorted fearful face and the mood dominating his most famous painting, *The Scream*. There is no doubt about what *The Scream* expresses, nor that it is a painting of the highest order, it is up there with van Gogh's corn fields and Picasso's *Guernica*. But a house painter on a ladder one fine day in the garden? The Impressionists elevated motifs such as this by capturing the moment in all its fullness and in that way tying the familiar and the everyday, that with which we are most intimate, to what lies just beyond the everyday and which one can sense on a summer day: that in the world which doesn't care about us, which doesn't care about anything, which merely exists, and which merely exists always – the eternal. There is nothing eternal about Munch's painter as he stands there on the ladder with a body made up of a couple of brushstrokes of white and beige, no eternity in the garden around him or in the barely glimpsed sky. No inner meaning, nor any meaning extracted from the external world – just a carelessly rendered scene of everyday life, verging on the insignificant in every direction.

Is this where sixty-four years of experience as a painter had brought him?

In a certain sense it was. Munch knew perfectly well how to paint a man on a ladder in a way that was photographic, realistic and anatomically correct – the studies he drew of the human body as a young man in Paris are technically perfect – he also knew well how to paint a man in a garden on a summer day impressionistically, and he presumably also knew how to paint the man on the ladder in a Munchian way. When he chose not to, it was because none of those techniques would help him accomplish what he was after. On the contrary, they would stand in his way.

But what was he after?

It can't have been much. It wasn't to create great art, it wasn't to paint a masterpiece, it was simply to capture the essence of this little scene. The essence of the house painter, which is the vertical arc of the body ending in the lifted hand holding the brush, the essence of the ladder, which is the slightly rickety horizontal steps, the essence of the flowers and the grass, which is their yellow and green colour. Munch must have been happy seeing the painter standing there, and he must have been happy painting him, for that is what the painting expresses, joy at the scene unfolding. Perhaps he also remembered another garden with a red building in the background which he once painted joyfully, in his youth?

There is something slightly humorous about the picture too, the small and crookedly set up ladder, the man's arm far above his head, while at the same time there is also a respect for the work, simply through the fact that Munch found the motif worthy of a painting, nothing elevated, just worthy of note. When we know that Munch was seventy-eight years old when he painted it and was considered to be beyond doubt his country's greatest artist, to many the very emblem of The Artist, it is difficult not to see the picture as an ironic comment on his own life's work. The man on the ladder is painting a house, Munch is painting a picture – what difference is there, really?

Munch painted a self-portrait at about the same time, it is one of his best-known pictures, it is entitled *Between the*

Clock and the Bed, and it is unlike almost all his other self-portraits in that he depicts himself humbly, as a humble man. He is standing between a clock with no hands and a bed, in front of a wall hung with pictures and paintings, of which some are recognisable as his own. His hands are down by his sides, in a neutral position verging on the subservient or self-effacing, it says, Here I am as I really am. His facial expression is also neutral, conveying neither affect nor inner drama. His gaze, which has been so central to his work and his position in the world, isn't visible, his eyes are almost entirely in shadow. It is as if he has positioned himself in front of us and in doing so is saying that this is all there is, this is me, neither more nor less.

Oh, how different it is from the self-portrait he made at the age of nineteen, which is so haughty! But also different from another late self-portrait, in which he is sitting in a chair with a blanket over his legs and turning his head towards us in a movement that is almost a snarl, odd because he is both exhibiting himself and guarding himself in one and the same motion. The man between the clock and the bed isn't guarding himself, he is just standing there, very erect.

Or the self-portrait from Ekely a few years earlier, where he is peering at the sun with paintbrush in hand and being the great painter, to say nothing of *Self-Portrait in Hell*, where he gives his own suffering biblical proportions. But this? An aged man standing very erect in his bedroom, dressed in a suit and shirt, as if to answer to death, which is evidently waiting just around the corner. Maybe it wasn't much, he seems to be saying, but it was still something! And there is plenty you don't know about me.

The picture of the house painter is not a self-portrait, but it invites reflection about what painting meant to Munch, through the difference between the man who is painting the house, there amid the world, and Munch, who is painting a picture of it, he too standing amid the world, but not *in* it in the same way, for while the colour with which the house painter coats the walls is also in the world, as matter, the colours which Munch lays upon the canvas in addition create another world. It is this world we see when we look at the picture. The connection between the two worlds can be more or less obvious, but Munch never let go of it, not even in his wildest experiments, and here it is as if the connection itself were the main thing, that the world in itself and the painting of it are placed side by side through the similarity between the two acts, the painter painting the house, Munch painting the picture. Unlike the self-portrait between the clock and the bed, this picture is full of the joy of living, humour and a faint undercurrent of melancholy. For although the painting in itself is insignificant and perhaps hardly worth a mention – it has never been exhibited – it is part of a clear and strong theme in Munch, of people working, people in nature, and these pictures are harmonious and beautiful – often the people are stretching their arms into the air, they are picking berries, they are lifting wooden planks, they are gripping branches, they are painting a house wall – and their faces are never visible, their identity is not what is important, not who they are but *that* they are, and that they merge with nature as a part of it.

These pictures are invariably melancholy, for they are always seen from a distance, the person seeing them is not there himself, is not himself part of the harmony, other than the one found in the act of painting itself, the only way of celebrating life that he knew, by turning away from it.

*

Some days before Christmas I drove to Malmö to pick up the picture I had bought. I thought the auction firm's offices lay in the centre of town, but the GPS on my mobile led me along railway tracks and past warehouses and workshops to a barrack-like building with a large gravelled yard outside. When it was my turn and the sales assistant fetched the picture from the storeroom and handed it to me, it was the first time I had held anything Munch had made: this he had had printed in Berlin and signed with a pencil in 1904, now I was holding it between my hands in an industrial area outside Malmö 112 years later.

I placed it on the back seat of the car with the lights from the windows shining in the darkness behind me, turned on the ignition and drove home with the roads full of cars just before the holiday.

It was a simple picture, but it was beautiful, and its aura was so strong that it took a long time to find a place for it on the wall where it didn't totally obliterate the other pictures hanging there.

Thousands of human faces are drawn around the world every day. Children do it all the time, and all art students, amateur artists and professionals. They draw the same thing: forehead, eyes, nose, mouth and chin. Cheeks, ears, hair. And it isn't difficult, all it takes is a little practice and a face emerges on the paper.

So what made this particular drawing unique?

For it was.

The amount of information had been reduced to a minimum, but without the presence of the face diminishing, on the contrary it was as if this gave it room to unfold in.

And that is what it's all about, isn't it? Presence? The presence of a human being, the presence of a landscape, the presence of a room, the presence of an apple – and the presence of the painting or drawing which lifts the human being, the landscape, the room, the apple to the fore.

In themselves pictures are beyond words, beyond concepts, beyond thought, they invoke the presence of the world on the world's terms, which also means that everything that has been thought and written in this book stops being valid the moment your gaze meets the canvas.

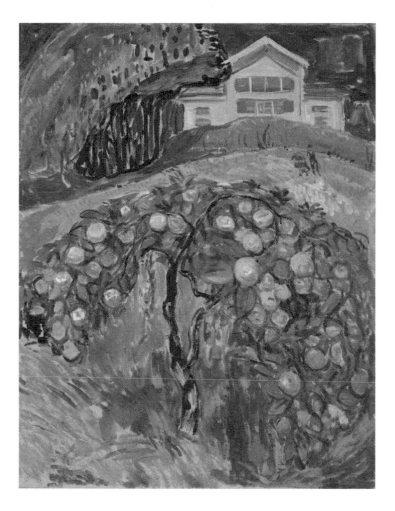

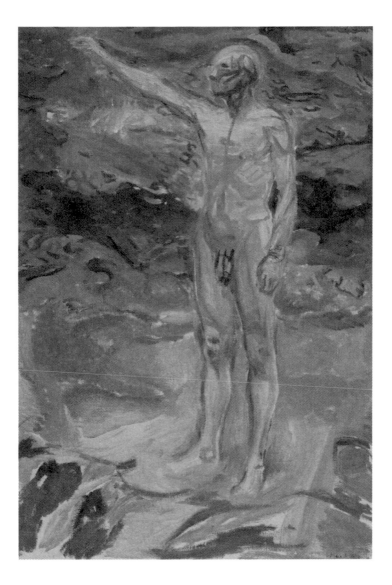

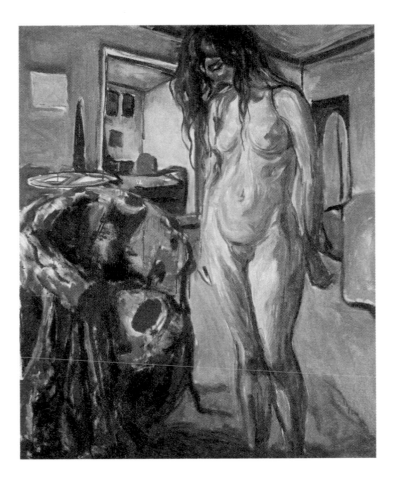

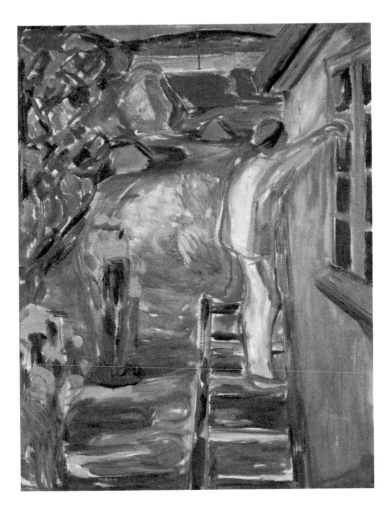

Notes

1. Gilles Deleuze, *Francis Bacon: The Logic of Sensation*, translated by Daniel W. Smith, London 2003.
2. MM.PN.858, Munch Museum, eMunch.no. Translation © Francesca M. Nichols.
3. MM.T.2734, Munch Museum, eMunch.no. Translation © Francesca M. Nichols.
4. Stian Grøgaard, *Edvard Munch: Et utsatt liv*, Oslo 2013, pp. 48–9.
5. Edvard Munch, *Livsfrisens tilblivelse*, Oslo *c.* 1928, MM.UT.13, Munch Museum, eMunch.no. Translation © Francesca M. Nichols.
6. Gilles Deleuze, 'Literature and Life', translated by Daniel W. Smith and Michael A. Greco, in *Critical Inquiry* Vol. 23, No. 2, 1997, University of Chicago Press.
7. Poul Erik Tøjner, *Munch: Med Egne Ord*, Oslo 2003, p. 43. Available in English, published with the title *Munch: In His Own Words*, translated by Jennifer Lloyd and Ian Lukins, London 2003.
8. Ibid. pp. 24–6.
9. MM.N.46, Munch Museum, eMunch.no. Translation © Francesca M. Nichols.

10. Ulrich Bischoff, *Edvard Munch: Images of Life and Death*, Cologne 2016, p. 63.
11. Edvard Munch, *Livsfrisens tilblivelse*.
12. Rolf Stenersen, *Edvard Munch: Close-up of a Genius*, translated and edited by Reidar Dittmann, Oslo 1994, p. 142.

Paintings

Unless otherwise stated, the paintings belong to the Munch Museum collection. Photographs © Munch Museum. All measurements in centimetres.

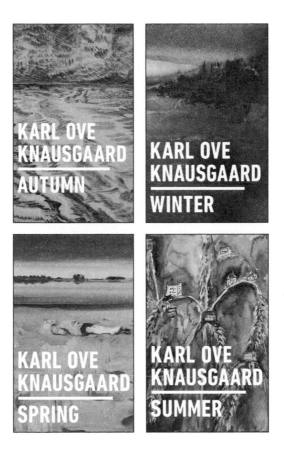
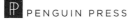 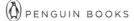